Achieving
QTS

Extending

Knowledge in Practice

Primary
English

Extending

Knowledge in Practice

Primary
English

David Wray
Jane Medwell

LearningMatters

First published in 2008 by Learning Matters Ltd.

British Library Cataloguing in Publication Data
A CIP record for this book is available from the British Library.

ISBN: 978 1 84445 104 3

Cover design by Topics – the Creative Partnership
Text design by Code 5 Design Associates Ltd
Project management by Deer Park Productions, Tavistock
Typeset by PDQ Typesetting Ltd, Newcastle under Lyme
Printed and bound in Great Britain by Bell & Bain Ltd, Glasgow

Learning Matters
33 Southernhay East
Exeter EX1 1NX
Tel: 01392 215560
info@learningmatters.co.uk
www.learningmatters.co.uk

Contents

Introduction

This book builds upon and extends our existing Learning Matters volume (Medwell, J., Moore, G., Wray, D. and Griffiths, V. (2007) 3rd edition, *Primary English: knowledge and understanding.* Exeter: Learning Matters). Its main aim is to provide you (as a trainee or newly qualified teacher) with a means to extend and deepen your command of the subject knowledge relevant to the teaching of English in primary schools, but in a manner which is designed to assist you to use such knowledge more actively in planning and implementing English lessons.

The context of the work

Since the publication and implementation of Circular 14/98, which laid down a set of national requirements for the training of teachers, there has been a demand for books expressly aimed at covering these requirements. There have been several phases in this demand.

Initially the concern was that the then National Curriculum for Initial Teacher Training delineated a list of key elements of subject knowledge in the core subjects which training institutions had to guarantee their trainees would be taught and, eventually, be competent in. Training providers were required to audit trainee subject knowledge and to provide opportunities for those trainees judged lacking in aspects of this knowledge to acquire it. To meet the demand for assistance with this aspect of primary teacher training, we produced, in 1997, *English for primary teachers: an audit and self-study guide* for Letts Educational. This was very much a 'quick and dirty' solution to the problem of trainee teacher subject knowledge – a problem which itself has changed significantly over the past ten years.

English for primary teachers allowed trainees to check their own knowledge of aspects of English and identify the areas they needed to work on if they were to meet the requirements for Qualified Teacher Status. It included a brief section on extending their knowledge but really this was quite limited.

In a partial attempt to remedy the latter deficiency of this book, in 2001 we produced the first edition of *Primary English: knowledge and understanding* for Learning Matters (the 3rd edition of this book, much updated, with several completely new chapters, was published in 2007 to coincide with the introduction of the new Standards for QTS). This book was and is a much fuller treatment of English subject knowledge and is intended to be used as a major textbook for courses of teacher training, a role it has fulfilled very successfully. It attempts to relate subject knowledge to classroom practice in teaching English in a much more extensive way than did its predecessor and many trainees have commented on how useful they have found this volume.

A new approach

However, the world moves on and, in 2008, we see the need for a rather different approach to developing the subject knowledge of trainee and newly qualified teachers. Both the previous volumes we have produced have been deliberately aimed at enhancing your substantive knowledge of aspects of English. Both have claimed to focus on knowledge which was directly relevant to classroom practice in teaching English, but in reality this was for both books a secondary consideration. The need now, as we see it, is to target a book directly at classroom practice in teaching English and, in the course of this, introduce and explain the subject knowledge you will need to teach effectively the material we suggest.

The aim of this new book is, therefore, to focus on teaching practice, including on the way several suggestions for teaching activities and sequences in primary English work. For each activity we suggest we have unpicked some of the subject knowledge with which you will need to be familiar in order to teach this activity successfully.

As well as this more practical approach, we have also aimed to make the new volume eminently readable. We are of the firm belief that good teachers of English, at whatever level but perhaps especially in primary schools, are those who are enthusiastic as well as knowledgeable about the subject. We hope in this volume to convey some of our own enthusiasm for English, its history and structure, to readers and, in turn, to you.

Book structure

The book consists of nine major chapters. In each chapter you will find:

- **suggestions for several lessons or teaching activities in English;**
- **some exploration of the subject knowledge background necessary to teach these lessons or activities successfully;**
- **a range of anecdotes and illustrations about English literature and language.**

The book does not attempt to be comprehensive in its treatment of subject knowledge in English. There are some aspects of this where, we would argue, there has already been rather too much advice given (teaching grammar comes into this category, we think). Rather, it takes an eclectic view of subject knowledge, choosing to focus on material which fascinates (and in many cases amuses) us.

The chapters cover the following material.

Chapter 1: Phonological awareness, language comprehension and knowledge about print. The teaching of early reading has changed significantly in the UK in the last two years, with much more emphasis being given to the teaching of phonics. You cannot, however, teach phonics without certain prerequisite knowledge in the children you teach, and in this chapter we explore this knowledge and how you might develop and assess it.

Chapter 2: Teaching phonics. There are a number of approaches to the teaching of phonics, with what is known as 'synthetic' phonics currently being the officially preferred method. In this chapter we explore approaches to teaching phonics and develop some of the understanding you will need in order to use these effectively.

Chapter 3: English vocabulary and the development of language. The English language: where has it come from and where is it going? Modern English cannot properly be understood without some understanding of its historical roots. How might an exploration of the history of English translate into useful classroom work?

Chapter 4: Looking closely at spelling. English spelling and English words can appear perverse yet an understanding of where these words derive from can make things a whole lot clearer both for teachers and for learners. In this chapter we will take a historical perspective on the development of English words and suggest ways in which primary pupils might investigate word development.

Chapter 5: Working with punctuation. Punctuation is often perceived as a set of rules that writers have to adhere to. In this chapter we will take a different approach, looking closely at a number of texts in which punctuation is used in ways that break some of our traditional 'rules'. These texts will be used as a starting point for teaching suggestions.

Chapter 6: Handwriting. Handwriting has definitely been the neglected part of literacy for a number of years. However, important new research has suggested that fluent and rapid handwriting can play a major role in the development of writing. In this chapter we explore what is currently known about handwriting and its teaching.

Chapter 7: Looking closely at reading comprehension. What do we do when we comprehend? In this chapter we explore some of the complex processes which are going on when readers try to understand what they are reading. Knowing what understanding involves is an important first step towards helping develop it.

Chapter 8: Approaches to developing comprehension. In this second, linked chapter, we explore some teaching strategies focused on the development of reading comprehension.

Chapter 9: New texts: new literacies. Texts are not what they were, and so reading and writing are also, therefore, not quite what they were. Teachers of English need to understand the nature and impact of textual variation in order to decide what they will teach to their pupils and how they might go about it.

1
Phonological awareness, language comprehension and knowledge about print

Chapter objectives

By the end of this chapter you should have developed your understanding of:

- **the importance of language comprehension and vocabulary development;**
- **the role and importance of phonological awareness;**
- **the importance of practitioner diagnosis and monitoring, as well as teaching.**

Professional Standards for QTS

Q14

Introduction

The simple view of reading (DfES, 2006) identifies language comprehension and word recognition as the two principal dimensions of reading development. Each of these dimensions of the reading process has its roots in the language experience of children before they begin formal phonics teaching and, often, before they begin school.

This chapter addresses what the Rose review (DfES, 2006) termed 'pre-reading' skills: the language comprehension, vocabulary growth and phonological awareness which underpin reading and phonics. These are the developmental outcomes of the 'broad and rich' language curriculum recommended by this review and, as such, are not just 'pre' reading – they are vital developmental steps towards literacy. Practitioners in the Foundation Stage need to understand the importance of this speaking and listening activity. It is the basis of not only language, but also future literacy development. Practitioners need to know what to observe and how to intervene to ensure children develop the phonological awareness and language comprehension which will carry them forward to become successful readers.

Learning about language in Early Years settings

Children coming into Early Years settings undergo a huge change in their experience of language use, new language variants and vocabulary and are asked to use their existing language in new ways.

Children coming into early childhood settings also experience different social uses of language from those they are used to at home. In the home, children talk to a very limited number of known adults who help them to make meaning. By knowing the child very well and being able to understand, interpret and extend utterances which would probably be unintelligible to an 'outsider', caregivers support young children learning to speak and listen. This is something of a contrast to the much less intimate relationships they will experience in

Early Years settings. So in these settings, children have to learn to listen to and understand new people and to talk to them clearly and audibly.

At home children are usually allowed to choose what they want to talk about and adults often follow their interests and elaborate upon them. In an Early Years setting, there will be a wide range of opportunities for talk about concrete experiences, stories, play and drama, but these may be very different from the talk topics they are used to in the home. The adults in such a setting may have less time to talk specifically to a particular child about a topic chosen by that child. This may be the first time a child has been addressed as part of a group or expected to follow rules about speaking. Getting other children of their own age to discuss with them may be a new and challenging experience. In such Early Years settings, children learn to attract and keep the attention of adults, to take turns and follow the 'rules' of different types of discussions, about new topics, using new vocabulary.

The type of language used in a setting may also be new to a child. In Early Years settings, many adults will use standard English and the words and syntax used by adults may be different from many children's home dialect or language. To use talk in a setting, children will learn new vocabulary and grammatical constructions as well as the rules and expectations of interaction with a wider range of people.

Learning to speak and listen in the more formalised, structured context of Early Years settings is, therefore, not a simple business, yet most children do manage to learn the patterns, language and expectations quite quickly. They do this by participating in play, drama, listening, manipulation and exploration and these experiences help them to learn the vocabulary and grammatical constructions used around and with them. This is what is meant by a 'broad and rich' language curriculum and it is the provision of this range of experiences and models which is the basis of vocabulary development and language comprehension. In this sort of setting practitioners will plan target vocabulary and talk experiences which engage children in speaking, listening, talk for communication and talk for thinking. The ways children respond to these opportunities will be the basis of assessments made by practitioners which will, ultimately, contribute to their Early Years Foundation (EYF) Profile. However, the incidental unplanned activities such as interaction between children, interaction between children and adults, listening to others playing are just as important in children's language development. A Foundation Stage setting is designed to stimulate and support talk.

In some settings teachers will use simple sign language (such as Makaton) as well as speaking clearly to children, especially when working in groups. By using signs for the key content words, practitioners give children additional support to comprehend target language. Sometimes, the use of sign language will be designed to support children with specific difficulties, but very often it is to help all the children engage with setting activity.

CASE STUDY CASE STUDY **CASE STUDY** CASE STUDY **CASE STUDY** CASE STUDY

This is an account of practice in a nursery with three- and four-year old children. The Ofsted report for this nursery suggests the children make excellent progress in their speaking and listening during their time there. The account is given by the setting leader.

When they come to the nursery, we have a real spread. At one end of the spectrum, some children are very confident and happy to speak to adults as soon as they start nursery. Of

course, this doesn't mean they can take turns, sustain a discussion or can talk with other children. At the other end of the spectrum we have some children who are practically silent for weeks after they come in. They may talk quietly to other children but won't talk to the adults unless approached. So we have to see progress individually. We spend time observing what they can do and giving them opportunities to speak in new situations.

In our nursery, there is no 'whole class' activity. We feel it is too daunting for this age group, but we are very keen for children to do activities and present ideas to their home group. Each week we plan for some target vocabulary related to our theme which will be used in a range of adult-led activities and plan a speaking and listening activity we would like them all to do – it is often about another area of the curriculum – explaining how the cornflour felt, or describing how they achieved something. Many of our children have English as their second or third language and we have some additional provision for them. As well as our target vocabulary, we identify an additional 'talk task' we aim to do with them each week. We also have an additional practitioner, part time, who helps them to negotiate child-led play activities.

One thing we tried, last year, was tracking individuals to monitor their speaking and listening. We observed each child for a session (two and a half hours) and made brief notes of what the child did and said under certain headings related to the curriculum guidance. Here is one example of notes made. This was very time consuming and we might only do this for a whole session if we are concerned about a child.

REFLECTIVE TASK

Compare the ways the staff in this setting have deliberately planned for the integration of speaking and listening into the curriculum they offer children with the approaches you have seen in other nursery settings.

Trees pre-school
Name: Mahdi   Age: 4.3   Languages: Farsi, English (little bit of Arabic)

Enjoy and use speaking in play
No talk during play with the water and then the cars. Brief bursts of play–not settled. Used 'give me', and 'need two' type requests and assurances to fellow builder over mobilo. Concentrated on this well and produced a recognisable car. Lots of shouting on the bikes – but not clear what – mostly clearing his path. Later, played silently with the sand – moving the cars. Concentrated hard

---

Talking to sort out ideas
'look', 'here' – one-word utterances over mobilo.

Imaginative and dramatic language
Outside play, joined in acting out Three little pigs (at adult instigation). Desperate to be the wolf and remembered huff and puff. Repeated whole refrain after adult and ran round repeating it.

Speaking clearly and audibly to others/Listening to others

When doing questions about the story (Three little pigs) in home group, seemed to listen to the others. Shook his head when he didn't agree with one child. Answered one question about the topic. 'Yes, please', 'no' and 'don't like it' (kiwi) over fruit. Didn't talk to the others.

Vocabulary range

Knew pigs, houses, but found it hard to repeat straw, bricks and wood when playing outside with adult-led group. Happy to play with the materials but not to discuss. Knew pear (not kiwi) and carrot.

Participation in group songs, rhymes, story, etc.

Joined in home group read of Three little pigs (also read yesterday). √ Keen. Answered question what is it about 'three pigs. building'. Joined in enthusiastically with the refrain 'I'll huff...etc.'
Action rhymes (short today). Did five little ducks clapping and acting. Could clap in time (five and little) but not keen to be a duck. 'No, please'

REFLECTIVE TASK

- **On the basis of these notes, what do you think are Mahdi's strengths in speaking and listening?**
- **Which area would you select for attention in working with Mahdi?**

Learning auditory discrimination

In Early Years settings we also expect children to develop totally new language skills – those of auditory analysis and reflection on language. These are skills which children have not needed in their daily lives but are vital in order for them to learn the key skills of word recognition and comprehension.

Discriminating sounds itself takes practice, and this is why Early Years practitioners take care to set up 'sound tables' or listening posts, where children can experiment with a range of instruments, or some sealed boxes with different contents which make interesting sounds. Exploring these helps children learn to listen to differences between sounds. Discussing them gives children new vocabulary and ideas. By doing discrimination activities with musical instruments or even interesting objects, practitioners can assess which children have developed sound awareness.

When children learn speech they gradually develop their store of words. First words appear at around a year, with a steady growth to a vocabulary of around 300 words by the age of three. However, children do not consciously analyse words: they learn meanings. So they may learn certain utterances as single words: 'stopit!' being the universal example. Children learn words as units of meaning in the stream of speech. They tend to learn 'content' words like nouns, verbs and adjectives first and 'structure' words like articles (*a, the, an*) and prepositions (*on, under, by*) later. In particular, they are not called on to reflect on what is and isn't a word until they begin to read and write when, by convention, we put spaces between the words. So discriminating words is an important skill which should be practised and developed across the Foundation and Key Stage 1 curriculum. These words – the sounds and meanings – are stored to be used for speaking and reading comprehension.

Learning phonological awareness

In preparing them to read, we ask children to analyse speech (aurally) below the level of words, which is totally new to them. Ultimately, we want children to be able to discriminate the phonemes in speech (phonemic awareness) and, at the first sign of this, teachers will begin phonics teaching. Discriminating phonemes, which are produced at the rate of around 900 per minute in normal speech and often have unclear boundaries, is a very advanced form of phonological awareness and there are a number of units children may learn to discriminate before they manage phonemes. It is the role of the Foundation Stage practitioner to give children practice in such discrimination and to monitor their development.

This is a well researched area and there is evidence (for example, Goswami and Bryant, 1990) that when children can discriminate words, the next unit they learn to discriminate is the syllable. A syllable can be defined in a number of ways, but is generally agreed to be a group of speech sounds (phonemes), usually including a vowel which constitutes a 'beat' in the rhythm of speech. This is why rhythm activities such as clapping names and short sentences, using shakers, bell and tambourines to follow the rhythm of songs, are so important. A key developmental question in phonological awareness is: can the child discriminate syllable rhythms?

The sort of evidence you might want to consider in judging this is whether he/she can clap the syllables in their name and the names of others and can clap, more or less reliably, simple rhythms in songs and rhymes. Children who can clap 'cat' as one beat, but 'kitten' as two may be ready to consider smaller units of sound; in particular, phonemes (the smallest units of sound in speech and the basis of phonics).

The developmental literature has identified further units of sound within syllables which children are most likely to discriminate. These are 'onsets' – usually the initial consonant phoneme of a syllable – and 'rimes' – usually the rest of the syllable including a vowel and consonant(s) (Goswami, 2002). However, these units are not taught to children. Instead, what we look for are children who can break single-syllable words down into parts or use alliteration. For instance, a child who can break *cat* into /c/ /at/ and *hat* into /h/ /at/ is clearly able to identify the initial phoneme in these words. The best way to address this is through repetitive sound games such as the 'pebble game', which involves sending a pebble round a group of children. Each child changes the onset phoneme of the single-syllable 'starter' word. So *cat* becomes *hat, bat, rat, gat, fat, bat*...

Identification of groups of final sounds – rhymes – is another important activity for promoting phonological awareness. Daily action rhymes, the use of rhyming stories and learning nursery rhymes by heart are all activities designed to promote rhyming. Discussing which words rhyme is also very useful. However, it is important to remember this is sound work and the skill is in listening to and discriminating final sound patterns, not looking at words written down. Again word games are the best way to assess this ability in children. For instance, show a child two objects from a selection (pin, pen, plug, tin, etc.). Ask the child to say the object names. Do they rhyme? Children select an object from a feelie bag (lid, jar, hat, duck, etc.) and have to think of a rhyming word. Can the child select rhyming words from their word store?

These aspects of phonological awareness – the abilities to discriminate sounds, words, syllables, onsets and rhymes – are important because, when children can do these, they are well prepared for a more focused programme of teaching phonics. If children can identify the beginning sound in *cat*, *ball*, *pig* and *Sam* and the rhymes in *bing* and *thing*, *their* and *care*, these children have probably developed the awareness of sound necessary to move on to a structured phonics programme which teaches them about the relationship between the smallest units of sound (phonemes) and the written units used to represent phonemes (graphemes).

CASE STUDY CASE STUDY **CASE STUDY** CASE STUDY **CASE STUDY** CASE STUDY

Ms B uses the first step of a commercial phonics package with her early Foundation Stage class, in the term before they go into their Reception year. It is an interactive whiteboard (IWB) package designed for teaching phonological awareness.

Each week I use one of the 'themes' – the zoo, the supermarket, etc. They fit into our general planning, and the scheme is designed so that they can be used in any order in Nursery. Each theme has a big, detailed picture which has sounds and animations. These are also a range of activities for the class or group, using the IWB. Using this package, I get children to pick out particular words and match them to objects. They can also pick out sounds and match them to the scenario. The activities are fun, for instance rhyming, where they select the object which rhymes with a given word or supply their own rhyming words. The rhythm activities get them to 'clap back' the rhythms of words about the theme. There is something for all the children and it is fun. Some children will only be able to pick out words or sounds, but most can do rhymes and rhythms (some are a bit intermittent) and a few can identify initial phonemes. The package also includes an alphabet element so we do letter formation and learn the alphabet before Reception in this school.

The IWB phonological awareness activities are enjoyable, quick and fit nicely into our day. I can do a group session in ten minutes or so and in that time all the children have really focused on listening, identifying sounds, rhymes and, in a few cases, phonemes. During the session, I can assess what the children can do although, ideally, one of the other staff will come and observe for me. We follow this up with object-based games at another time in the week.

This package also has independent computer activities for children to do each week, related to the theme. These are put out as a free choice activity and are really popular. I have been surprised how often pairs of children will do them on the computer, chattering away as they go. I sometimes think that it is the best talk toy we have.

REFLECTIVE TASK

Consider:

- **what phonological awareness assessment opportunities does such a discrete teaching session offer?**
- **what activities could you do without an interactive whiteboard to offer a similar session?**

Learning phonemic discrimination

One aspect of the ability to discriminate different types of sounds, discussed above, is the ability to discriminate phonemes – the smallest units of sound in speech. This is called phonemic discrimination. This is probably the last unit children will be able to discriminate because it means separating spoken words into quite subtle units. So *cat* has three phonemes /c/ /a/ /t/ but *church* also has three phonemes /ch/ /ur/ /ch/. There is some evidence that not all phonemes have the same saliency for young children. Those phonemes which are onsets or rimes are easier to learn (Goswami, 2002), so it may make sense to draw attention to the beginnings and ends of words, emphasising alliteration and rhyme. Activities which do this, including action rhymes, tongue-twisters and the sort of play activities illustrated in Phase 1 of the Letters and Sounds materials, allow the practitioner to engage children in discrimination activities and make assessments of developing phonemic awareness. Early phonemic awareness is about discrimination of sounds, not (yet) of spellings, but there is some evidence that becoming aware of how the alphabetic code works through working with print helps children to develop phonemic awareness. This is discussed below.

The experiences discussed above, such as rhymes, songs, and object games, all contribute to children learning to perceive phonemes in speech. However, some of the activities which make the greatest contribution will be unexpected, such as children writing messages or notices. These activities motivate very young children to really listen to and break down sounds in speech, even before they are being taught these relationships formally. Every nursery setting should offer children the chance to write freely.

Learning about print

This chapter, so far, has concentrated on children's learning of language comprehension, forms of talk and analysis of the structures of speech. At the same time as children in the nursery are learning this, they will also be learning about the basic conventions of print and written texts. These include:

- **directionality – that writing goes from left to right;**
- **a concept of word – that there are spaces between words and a spoken word can be written down (and vice versa);**
- **permanence – that when you write a message it has the same content every time it is read;**
- **alphabet knowledge (which is discussed in more detail below).**

For children to learn these things they need to see much more than books and the Foundation Stage setting is usually not only full of print, but is also a place for children to see writing being done and read. Some examples follow.

- **Name cards. These are often children's first recognised words and can be used as a mechanism for choosing an activity, for reserving a place or for signing in at the start of a session. Name cards can be traced and copied.**
- **Signs and labels. These can be used for equipment, for personal possessions, for basic rules, for displays. It is important to create these with the children and read them with the children. Otherwise, they are just decoration.**
- **Play media. Any dramatic play setting (home, shop, cafe, post office, etc.) has a literacy component. They all need certain signs and offer opportunities for writing. Practitioners can model using some of these, but must recognise that children may want to use them differently.**
- **Reading or writing with a small group of children, using a big book or large sheet of paper. These activities need to involve the children in suggesting topics, details, etc., and happen often.**

The key issue in planning these opportunities is that you cannot assume that by putting up a display, a child will notice or engage with it. You need to place it strategically, point it out and show children how (and why) to engage with it. Children also need to see reading and writing happening – not just the products. If you want children to read and write they need to see how you actually do it. This means that it is better for you to read the story than play a tape. It is better for you to write up a list on a flipchart than have it prepared and typed out.

One important part of learning about print is learning the alphabet in order and the names of the letters. This is not, at first, directly related to children's developing phonological awareness; it is the rote learning of the names of letters and their associated shape. However, alphabetic knowledge is associated with success at learning to read. This is one of the easiest pieces of knowledge to teach – sing the alphabet song and play letter-recognition games to learn letter names. Although some teachers worry that knowing letter names may confuse children about to embark on phonics learning, the opposite is true. If a child can name *c* and *h*, then they can discuss the digraph *ch* without resorting to incorrect sounding of /c/ and /h/. Knowing the alphabet is great preparation for phonics and also teaches children one of the most common organising systems in the world.

As children are learning letter names, it is also a good time to begin learning the motor patterns associated with good letter formation. Lots of air writing, chalks on tarmac, paint and play are a good start.

Learning about reading and writing

Perhaps the most important insight about literacy for every child is that reading and writing have a number of purposes that are relevant to them. The child who learns that if you give an adult a book you get a fun story or rhyme, has learnt one of the most important lessons about reading. By having regular story reading, story telling, rhyme times, story-linked play and drama activities, children learn why you (and they) read. At the same time, of course, you might also be teaching them something about social behaviour, knowledge and understanding of the world or anything else the books contain. The non-fiction purposes of reading and writing are just as much fun. If the child can pick from a fruit 'menu' at snack time, sign up for an activity by writing their name (or a form of it), or read the signs and magazines in a dramatic play area, they can understand the purpose and relevance of reading for them. Many of the best opportunities for this learning do not require much teaching: book browsing, for instance, is more a question of displaying a group of enticing texts.

PRACTICAL TASK PRACTICAL TASK **PRACTICAL TASK** PRACTICAL TASK **PRACTICAL TASK**

One of the most obvious activities for teaching about print is reading a big book with a group of children. By using a pointer as you read, the directionality of print is emphasised. If you ask children to pick out a word or to predict the next word, you emphasise spoken to written word correspondence. By re-reading all or part of the text, you teach children about the permanence of writing. However, shared reading is not the only opportunity for children to learn these important concepts. List all the reading and writing opportunities in your Early Years setting which help children to learn these concepts.

How many reading/writing opportunities or models would you expect one child to encounter in a nursery session?

Observe one child for a nursery session and make notes about his/her talk and engagement with print, under the headings below.

- **Talking to communicate**
- **Talking to sort out ideas**
- **Imaginative and dramatic language**
- **Speaking clearly and audibly to others/Listening to others**
- **Vocabulary range**
- **Language analysis in group songs, rhymes, story, etc. (rhythm, rhyme, etc.)**
- **Involvement in reading and writing**
- **Using reading/writing for a purpose (enjoyment, task selection, etc.)**

A SUMMARY OF **KEY POINTS**

> **Language comprehension and word recognition are two key dimensions of reading development and both begin in speaking and listening activity.**

> **Just by taking part in an Early Years setting, young children learn new vocabulary, syntax, uses for talk and patterns of talk. They need a balanced range of talk activities to learn all types of talking.**

> **Auditory analysis of language is a totally new skill for most children coming into education, which will prepare them for the phonics (word-identification) part of the reading process.**

> **Young children need to discriminate sounds, words, rhythms, rhymes and, eventually, phonemes. They can do this through structured playful activities.**

> **Young children can and should learn the alphabet and letter names.**

> **Practitioners in the early Foundation Stage can help children learn key insights about print through engaging them with stories, signs, reading and writing.**

> **Children need to learn why reading (and writing) is worth doing.**

> **All these points contribute to the broad and rich language environment children need to learn literacy.**

Moving on

Phonological awareness is a developmental issue for children but it is only the beginning of phonics teaching. The government programme Letters and Sounds includes exciting, interactive phonological awareness activities as Phase 1 of the programme. See the next chapter for discussion of phonics teaching, the next step in reading and writing. Likewise, print awareness will be accompanied (hopefully) by mark making and writing, which can reveal a good deal about children's understandings about language.

REFERENCES REFERENCES **REFERENCES** REFERENCES **REFERENCES** REFERENCES

DfES (2006) *Independent review of the teaching of early reading* (The Rose review). Available online at *www.standards.dfes.gov.uk/rosereview/finalreport*

Goswami, U (2002) Phonology, reading development, and dyslexia: a cross linguistic perspective. *Annals of Dyslexia*, 52: 141–63

Goswami, U and Bryant, P (1990) *Phonological skills and learning to read*. London: Lawrence Erlbaum

FURTHER READING FURTHER READING **FURTHER READING** FURTHER READING

PNS/DfES (2007) *Letters and sounds: notes of guidance for practitioners and teachers*. DfES. This is the government-funded programme for phonics and includes a substantial amount of phonological and phonemic awareness material in Phase 1. The video exemplification and practitioner notes are very helpful.

DfES/PNS (2006) *The Primary Framework for literacy and mathematics: core position papers underpinning the renewal of guidance for teaching literacy and mathematics*. London: DfES. Available online at *http://www.standards.dfes.gov.uk/primary/features/primary/pri_fwk_corepapers/pri_fwk_corepapers_0385506.pdf*

DfES/PNS (2007) *Framework for teaching literacy and mathematics*. London: DfES. Available online at *http://www.standards.dfes.gov.uk/primaryframeworks/literacy/*

Dombey, H and Moustafa, M (1998) *Whole to part phonics*. London: CLPE

2
Teaching phonics

Chapter objectives

By the end of this chapter you should have developed your understanding of:

- **what constitutes phonics teaching and its place in the literacy curriculum;**
- **recent recommendations and direction of current phonics teaching;**
- **subject knowledge for phonics teaching;**
- **key approaches to phonics teaching.**

Professional Standards for QTS

Q14

Introduction

Few would deny that knowing the alphabetic patterns of English is an advantage for anyone wanting to read or write the language and should be an entitlement for all children. This is the role of phonics – to teach children to use the alphabetic patterning of English to read and spell. Phonics is not a subject in itself – it is a part of reading and writing. As teachers we aim to teach children to use the knowledge and skills of phonics rapidly and automatically to read and write. By mastering the necessary knowledge and skills early, children are freed up to use their reading and writing for thinking and learning. However, this is not to say that children should only learn phonics in the early stages of their literacy careers. Reading and writing are much more complex processes than simply decoding and recoding and so phonics learning is set into a whole network of other literacy practices which teach children about the purposes, uses, practices, meanings and understandings that are part of reading and writing. This chapter concentrates on phonics teaching but it is important that this is set into a broad and balanced literacy curriculum. Phonics without stories, rhymes, book browsing, shared reading, mark making and labelling would be abstract, useless stuff.

Enquiries into the teaching of phonics have recently reported in a number of English-speaking countries. In the United States, the National Reading Panel investigated the research into the teaching of reading (NRP, 2000); in Australia the *Teaching reading review and recommendations* (DEST, 2004) was the result of a national review into the teaching of literacy; and in England the *Independent review into the teaching of early reading* (DfES, 2006) (The Rose review) has reported 'best practice in teaching early reading and phonics'. All three reports strongly recommended an integrated approach to reading which teaches oral language, vocabulary, phonics and comprehension. All three reports also recommended phonics within a broad and rich literacy curriculum. In this chapter we concentrate on the most recent approach to teaching phonics, advocated by the Rose review (DfES, 2006) and built into the Framework for teaching literacy (DfES/PNS, 2007), the Early Years Foundation Stage (EYFS) (DCSF, 2007) and the Letters and sounds phonics programme (PNS/DfES, 2007).

What is phonics?

The publication of the Rose review gave phonics a new status and position within the National Curriculum, stating that: *the National Curriculum treats phonic work as essential content for learning, not a method of teaching. How schools should teach that content is a matter of choice.*

Whether to teach phonics is not a matter for choice by schools or teachers. As the Rose review emphasises: *All maintained schools with primary aged pupils are required to teach phonics, the content of which is prescribed as knowledge, skills and understanding in the statutory National Curriculum programmes of study for English, for pupils from the age of five.* Phonics has certainly grown in scope. But what does this include? The Rose review specifies core knowledge and skills.

Children must be taught:

- **grapheme/phoneme (letter/sound) correspondences (the alphabetic principle) in a clearly defined, incremental sequence;**
- **to apply the highly important skill of blending (synthesising) phonemes in order, all through a word to read it;**
- **to apply the skills of segmenting words into their constituent phonemes to spell;**
- **that blending and segmenting are reversible processes.**

The Key Stage 1 National Curriculum states that at the end of Key Stage 1 children should be taught to:

- **identify and respond to sound patterns in language (for example, alliteration, rhyme, word play);**
- **sound and name the letters of the alphabet;**
- **link sound and letter patterns, exploring rhyme, alliteration and other sound patterns;**
- **identify syllables in words;**
- **recognise that the same sounds may have different spellings and that the same spellings may relate to different sounds;**
- **write each letter of the alphabet;**
- **use their knowledge of sound–symbol relationships and phonological patterns (for example, consonant clusters and vowel phonemes);**
- **write familiar words and attempt unfamiliar ones.**

To this, the recommendations of the Rose review also add the reading of some irregular (termed 'tricky') words which are not phonically predictable.

Phonics today includes the development of phonological awareness (discussed in the previous chapter), the knowledge of sound – symbol correspondences, knowledge of the alphabet and names of letters, the skills of blending and segmenting, and, rather strangely, sight knowledge of common irregular words and their spellings. The Letters and sounds programme (PNS/DfES, 2007) also adds some morphemic content at the later stages, so that children learn common spelling patterns such as *–ed* endings (which are phonically irregular for historical reasons.)

All this detail gives us a clear, statutory picture of what we must teach children under the heading 'phonics', but the nature of that teaching remains a choice for schools. It is about this aspect of phonics, the choice of teaching method, that the debates of recent years have raged.

Synthetic or analytic phonics?

The most recent debate has been about the type of phonics teaching which should be undertaken. Older government programmes (such as Progression in phonics) emphasised analytic phonics, where children identify phonemes in whole words and segment the words into phonemes. These programmes also ask learners to analyse other words with similar characteristics and look at word patterns and families (*c-ake, t-ake*, etc.). Older programmes introduced new grapheme-phoneme correspondences gradually and some of them introduced the consonants before vowels, as onset consonants are easier for children to discriminate. This meant that children did not start blending and segmenting words for some considerable time.

In synthetic programmes (such as Letters and sounds) children are systematically taught the phonemes associated with particular graphemes. Children are taught these at a fast rate, usually four or more phonemes each week. Synthetic programmes demand that children blend phonemes to make words and segment words into phonemes right from the beginning of their structured phonics programme. For this reason, synthetic programmes introduce consonants and vowels right from the start of the structured programme and children blend and segment consonant-vowel-consonant (CVC) words from the start. Synthetic programmes emphasise the use of decodable texts (that is, those containing phonically regular words) and some of the more extreme programmes do not favour other reading strategies or high-frequency non-regular words in the early stages of reading.

Many teachers have used elements of both synthetic and analytic approaches and both approaches have advocated stimulating and active multi-sensory teaching in recent years. However, proponents of different programmes have made claims about improved effectiveness of one type of instruction over another. A recent Scottish study involving 300 children compared analytic and synthetic approaches. The authors concluded that *the synthetic phonics approach, as part of the reading curriculum, is more effective than the analytical phonics approach* (Johnson and Watson, 2005, p9). However, the rigour and methods of this small study have been heavily criticised (Lewis and Ellis, 2006). A systematic review of the research findings on the use of phonics in the teaching of reading and spelling (Torgerson et al., 2006) found only three randomised control trials in this area and concluded that there was no statistically significant difference in effectiveness between synthetic and analytic phonics instruction. However, the Torgerson review (as well as the Australian reading review and the American National Reading Panel) confirmed that *systematic phonics instruction within a broad literacy curriculum was found to have a statistically significant positive effect on reading accuracy* (2006, p9). A synthetic approach works – but we do not know whether it works better than any other approach. The Rose review stated that it could not wait for the results of long-term research studies and stated that *Having considered a wide range of evidence, the review has concluded that the case for systematic phonic work is overwhelming and much strengthened by a synthetic approach*. This finding may not be well founded in research evidence but it is a key statement in establishing a change in policy and it will be interesting to see whether this change in approach is important in improving reading and spelling standards. For this reason, this chapter concentrates on the recommendations in implementing such a phonics programme.

First, choose your programme

One of the key thrusts of the Rose recommendations was that schools should select and work to a (synthetic) phonics programme. However, this does not imply that it would be sufficient to continue to use one of the older, analytic based programmes. To guide schools in choosing a structured and possibly synthetic programme the DfES provided core criteria for selection of a programme. Such a programme should:

- present high-quality systematic phonic work, as defined by the independent review of teaching of early reading and now encapsulated in the Primary Framework, as the prime approach to decoding print;
- enable children to start learning phonic knowledge and skills systematically by the age of five with the expectation that they will be fluent readers, having secured word-recognition skills by the end of Key Stage 1;
- be designed for the teaching of discrete, daily sessions progressing from simple to more complex phonic knowledge and skills and covering the major grapheme-phoneme correspondences;
- enable children's progress to be assessed;
- use a multi-sensory approach so that children learn variously from simultaneous visual, auditory and kinaesthetic activities which are designed to secure essential phonic knowledge and skills;
- demonstrate that phonemes should be blended, in order, from left to right, 'all through the word' for reading;
- demonstrate how words can be segmented into their constituent phonemes for spelling and that this is the reverse of blending phonemes to read words;
- ensure children apply phonic knowledge and skills as their first approach to reading and spelling even if a word is not completely phonically regular;
- ensure that children are taught high-frequency words that do not conform completely to grapheme-phoneme correspondence rules;
- ensure that, as early as possible, children have opportunities to read texts (and spell words) that are within the reach of their phonic knowledge and skills even though every single word in the text may not be entirely decodable by the children unaided.

Many commercially available programmes and Letters and sounds, the PNS programme, meet these criteria. Indeed, it would be perfectly possible for a school to design its own programme to meet these criteria using a range of commercial and home-made materials. The Rose review cautioned against a 'pick and mix' approach, not because there is any robust evidence that one programme is better than another, but because it is not the programme which does the teaching. A programme is merely a structured set of agreed teaching points. Any good phonics programme includes:

- a range of phonological awareness games and activities;
- an agreed order and pace of introduction of phoneme-grapheme correspondences (including consonants and vowels from the outset);
- blending and segmenting from the beginning of phoneme-grapheme introductions;
- an agreed range of activities and lesson pattern which all teachers can use;
- a set of agreed terminology for all staff, parents and children to use about phonics;
- training materials so that everyone has the same subject knowledge;
- assessment and recording advice.

It is how you use these ingredients to teach – consistently, regularly, with enthusiasm and commitment – that ensures the success of your phonics programme. Really, whether /s/ is introduced in week 1 or week 2 has no magic value at all. But it will make a great difference to examples of blending you can use when planning your teaching for those weeks and, if you use examples which include unknown graphemes, you will confuse children. Whichever order of introduction of phoneme-grapheme correspondences you use, you will need to have a great many examples of words which use only those phonemes and graphemes for use in lessons. This is where a prepared programme is helpful. Progression and continuity are built into a programme and this means that children will continue with the phonics programme and learn more than just the most basic grapheme-phoneme correspondences.

One useful aspect of being 'on-programme' is the shared expectation and experience of the children, parents and staff involved. If all staff have trained for a new programme together, you will have a shared vocabulary. Do staff in your school say 'sound' or 'phoneme', 'consecutive consonants' or 'consonant cluster'? It doesn't matter as long as you all say the same thing and mean the same thing. If the Reception and Key Stage 1 classes all use a certain pattern of teaching phonics, then children know what to expect and teachers can change classes with minimal disruption. Most importantly of all, if you have chosen and trained to use a particular programme as a staff, you are likely to do so with enthusiasm and consistency.

CASE STUDY CASE STUDY CASE STUDY CASE STUDY CASE STUDY CASE STUDY

Gina is the literacy co-ordinator in a suburban primary school. She has been working on the school's phonics programme.

We put a lot of effort into phonics only four years ago – making resources and games. I thought we didn't need to make changes, really, until I did the Letters and sounds training offered to all schools. I realised at once that we didn't do enough sound awareness work in Nursery and Reception and that the order in which we introduced phonemes didn't allow early blending. I was rather sceptical about whether children could learn new phonemes at the pace proposed. Still, I could see we needed a new programme and everyone needed to understand it.

I worked with a team and, eventually, we decided not to use Letters and sounds because we felt it demanded so much preparation of resources in the later phases. We have gone for an electronic whiteboard-based commercial phonics programme which has masses of material and is very visual. We have added lots of the Letters and sounds activities to it to make the sessions more active and still use the reading books we already have, which are quite strongly patterned. So far it has been really interesting. The children coped with the pace of learning brilliantly and I think all the sound awareness in Nursery is paying off.

The training for everyone is a real challenge because you can't just grab all the training time. It is already planned for and, actually, numeracy is our school focus. So far we have done one half-day training with the electronic phonics materials that come with our new programme and three staff meetings. One of these just focused on pronouncing the phonemes and learning the phonics vocabulary. The next was on lesson structure, another about assessment in lessons. Next year we have planned two more meetings about working with children who are struggling to keep up with the class and about including phonics in shared and guided reading. I will be doing observations of phonics teaching throughout FKS and KS1 and offering support. It will take at least until the end of next year to feel we are really happy with the new programme but we have worked hard and the children and parents like our new materials. We are doing a parent workshop next term for the new parents.

Consider these questions.

- **What issues affected Gina's choice of programme?**
- **Who needs to be involved in a change of phonics programme?**
- **What training would you need to use a new phonics programme?**

Know your subject

Phonics is a small but technical part of reading and it is essential that everyone involved knows their subject knowledge and how to talk about it. Teachers, teaching assistants, parents and children need to share these understandings if phonics teaching is to be successful. Key areas of knowledge you should have include:

- children's development in phonological and phonemic awareness;
- a progression in phonic knowledge and skills;
- correct pronunciation of phonemes;
- a vocabulary for phonics teaching;
- knowledge of your school programme and policy;
- knowledge about recommended lesson structures;
- knowledge of your children and their needs and progress.

Children's development in phonological and phonemic awareness

This was discussed in the previous chapter, but it is important to establish that children embarking on structured phonics proper do have phonemic awareness. *Unless you have phonemic awareness... it is impossible to gain much from instruction in phonics* (Harrison, 2004, p41). Although the Rose review insisted that structured phonics instruction should begin by age five, it is interesting to note that most of the research on phonics teaching has been done with children aged six or seven. It is also important to recognise that at four or five, many children cannot hear or pronounce some of the consonant phonemes (MacCartney, 2006) for perfectly normal developmental reasons. There is also a high level of intermittent hearing loss suffered by young children who catch colds during their Early Years education. These factors mean that teachers need to decide when children are ready to start a structured phonics programme.

A progression in phonic knowledge and skills

This is the basis of phonics teaching and has been included in the Early Years Foundation Stage (DCSF, 2007) and the Framework for teaching literacy (PNS/DFES, 2007) in its own special strand – Strand 5 – word recognition, which ends at Year 2. This is an important issue. The phonics strand ends at Year 2 because phonics is a time-limited strategy. Use of phonics for writing and reading is an extremely useful 'leg up' for reading and writing, even with the 'deep orthography' (Dombey, 2006) of English where letters do not simply represent sounds. However, there are also other, competing, patterns in English and it is important that, by the end of Year 2, children know that using sound-symbol correspondences is not enough to read and write fluently and automatically and that children have additional strategies. Teaching these strategies (such as the visual patterns in spelling) can compete with phonics teaching, so phonics needs to be addressed, and become automatic, early.

A great deal of phonics learning takes place in the Early Years Foundation Stage. The requirement for children to *Explore and experiment with sounds, words and text* (DfES, 2006) refers to the phonological development discussed in the previous chapter. In addition, in the EYFS, the Framework says children should:

- link sounds to letters, naming and sounding the letters of the alphabet;
- hear and say sounds in words in the order in which they occur;
- read simple words by sounding out and blending the phonemes all through the word from left to right;
- recognise common digraphs;
- use phonic knowledge to write simple regular words and make phonetically plausible attempts at more complex words;
- read a range of familiar and common words and simple sentences independently;
- read texts compatible with their phonic knowledge and skills;
- read and write one grapheme for each of the 44 phonemes;
- read some high-frequency words;
- use a pencil and hold it effectively to form recognisable letters, most of which are formed correctly.

If children are to know all 44 phonemes and be able to blend and segment them, they need rapid introduction of the phonemes, including consonants and short vowels in their Reception year. There is no correct order of introduction, and each programme will use a slightly different order. You need to know the order of introduction of your programme if you are to plan examples for your teaching.

PRACTICAL TASK PRACTICAL TASK **PRACTICAL TASK** PRACTICAL TASK **PRACTICAL TASK**

Here is a typical progression in the introduction of phoneme-grapheme correspondences in Reception.

Week	Graphemes/phonemes to be taught
1	a t s p
2	c/k o m g
3	h i n r
4	e d u f
5	b l j w
6	sh ai oa ee
7	ch or y ng
8	v oo OO z
9	x th TH ie
10	qu ou oi er
11	ue ar nk ck

You can see that the short vowels and consonants spelt with a single-letter grapheme are generally taught first. This teacher aims to teach four phonemes and graphemes each week and use the last daily phonemes session of the week to consolidate the new information.

If you were planning a consolidation lesson for Week 6, which of these words would you be able to use?

win, bow, bed, chip, sat, flush, pug, red, pan, pay, kit, egg, king, pain, run, sheep, main, bin, safe, kite, get, she, boat, reef, meet, job, blush, dunk

Which words contain unknown phonemes?
Which words contain unknown graphemes?
Which words are not CVC (consonant-vowel-consonant) words?
Which words contain the split digraph?

The answers are at the end of the chapter, but if you have difficulty with any of these issues, we suggest you look at *Primary English, knowledge and understanding* 3rd edition (Medwell et al, 2007). Are there any words which you consider unsuitable because they are outside a five year old's vocabulary range?

In addition to introducing these phonemes, blending and segmenting, teachers also need to teach common 'sight' or 'tricky' words, like *go*, *to*, *the*.

Phonics does not end with CVC words and one representation of each phoneme. At Year 1 a great deal more is asked of children. For example:

- **recognise and use alternative ways of pronouncing the graphemes already taught, for example, that the grapheme 'g' is pronounced differently in 'get' and 'gem'; the grapheme 'ow' is pronounced differently in 'how' and 'show';**
- **recognise and use alternative ways of spelling the phonemes already taught, for example that the /ae/ sound can be spelt with 'ai', 'ay' or 'a-e'; that the /ee/ sound can also be spelt as 'ea' and 'e'; and begin to know which words contain which spelling alternatives;**
- **identify the constituent parts of two-syllable and three-syllable words to support the application of phonic knowledge and skills;**
- **recognise automatically an increasing number of familiar high-frequency words;**
- **apply phonic knowledge and skills as the prime approach to reading and spelling unfamiliar words that are not completely decodable;**
- **read more challenging texts which can be decoded using their acquired phonic knowledge and skills, along with automatic recognition of high-frequency words;**
- **read and spell phonically decodable two-syllable and three-syllable words.**

To achieve these goals children need to learn to blend and segment consecutive consonants (sp, sl, str) and to know a range of graphemes for the same phoneme. Polysyllabic words present particular challenges as so many of them, when pronounced, include the unstressed vowel known in English as 'schwa'. This is the /uh/ sound usually made by a vowel in an unstressed syllable of spoken English, for example: the, a, often, broken, roller, pillar, motor, famous, favour, murmur, about, cotton, mountain, happen, centre, picture, cupboard. As you can see, schwa can be spelled in many different ways and it is difficult to find patterns. Often, a learning visual pattern or word family is the best guide in these words.

In Year 2 the word-recognition requirements of Strand 5 of the Primary Framework include learning the less common graphemes, although the usefulness of these less common patterns has been questioned (Solity, 2006). The bulk of this strand focuses on automatic use of phonics for reading and spelling and the use of other strategies like sight words and spelling patterns, which are usually visual rather than phonic. In Year 2, children learn common morphemes like –ed and –ing and how to chink words and use morphemic and etymological information as well as visual patterns for spelling.

- Read independently and with increasing fluency longer and less familiar texts.
- Spell with increasing accuracy and confidence, drawing on word recognition and knowledge of word structure, and spelling patterns.
- Know how to tackle unfamiliar words that are not completely decodable.
- Read and spell less common alternative graphemes including trigraphs.
- Read high- and medium-frequency words independently and automatically.

PRACTICAL TASK PRACTICAL TASK PRACTICAL TASK PRACTICAL TASK PRACTICAL TASK

Complete this cloze procedure.

The alphabet contains 26 _____. In spoken English there are around _____ phonemes, depending on your _____.

A phoneme is the smallest unit of _____ in speech. Each phoneme can be represented by one or more _____. A grapheme may have one or more _____. Graphemes with two letters are called _____. Graphemes with ___ letters are trigraphs. Each grapheme can represent one or more _____.

There are two main types of _____: consonants and vowels. The _____ or so consonants are made by impeding the flow of air through the mouth and nose with the lips, tongue, teeth and palate. Vowels are generally divided into short and _____ vowel phonemes.

Early phonics teaching focuses on consonant, _____, _____ words, then moves on to more complicated structures including consecutive _____. Eventually, alternative _____ for each phoneme are learnt and alternative phonemes for each grapheme.

The answers are at the end of the chapter. If you have any difficulty with these basic terms, you might want to consult *Primary English: teaching theory and practice* 3rd edition (Medwell et al, 2007).

Correct pronunciation of phonemes

This is a relatively simple but surprisingly important issue. If consonants are pronounced in an exaggerated way, it is tempting to add a schwa sound to make the consonant easier to hear: /cuh/ rather than /c/. This can make it very hard for children to blend or segment the words accurately. The sounds which are particularly difficult to pronounce without the dreaded schwa are c, t, b, p and g. Practice these, using a video model if necessary. A DVD containing a practice session has been included in the Letters and sounds package sent to all schools. It is important that everyone involved in phonics teaching knows this pronunciation and the inclusion of phoneme practice has become a common (if slightly bizarre) practice in parent workshops for reception parents.

A vocabulary for phonics teaching

This is equally important. Adults and children alike know what they are discussing and avoid inconsistency. This includes using letter names when appropriate. The digraph ch is spelt c ('see') h ('aich') – it is not spelt /c/ ('cuh') /h/ ('huh'). By using phonemes to 'spell out' digraphs, you teach children practices which are simply incorrect and confusing.

REFLECTIVE TASK

REFLECTIVE TASK

Complete your school glossary of phonics vocabulary by deleting words you do not use. You should have one term for each concept and use it consistently. This means you should not use alternatives, which confuse children.

Phoneme or **sound**. The smallest unit of sound in a word that can change its meaning.

Grapheme or **spelling of a phoneme**. A grapheme is a letter or group of letters representing a phoneme. There is always the same number of graphemes in a word as phonemes.

Letter. The alphabet contains 26 letters.

Grapheme–phoneme correspondences (GPCs) or **sound-symbol correspondence** (SSC). We convert graphemes to phonemes when we are reading aloud (decoding written words). We convert phonemes to graphemes when we are spelling (encoding words for writing). To do this, children need to learn which graphemes correspond to which phonemes and vice versa.

Segment [verb] or **break down**. To break a word into its constituent phonemes.

Blend [verb] or **run together** or **synthesise**. To build words from their constituent phonemes to read.

Digraphs and **trigraphs** (and four-letter graphemes). A digraph is a two-letter grapheme where two letters represent one sound, such as 'ea' in *seat* and 'sh' in *ship*. A trigraph is a three-letter grapheme where three letters represent one phoneme (e.g. 'eau' in *bureau*, and 'igh' in *night*).

Split digraph or **magic e** has a letter that splits, i.e. comes between, the two letters in the digraph, as in *make* and *take*.There are six split digraphs in English spelling: 'a-e', 'e-e', 'i-e', 'o-e', 'u-e', 'y-e', as in *make, scene, like, bone, cube, type*.

A very few words have more than one letter in the middle of a split digraph (e.g. *ache, blithe, cologne, scythe*).

Knowledge of your school programme and policy

You can only teach phonics if you know your school policy and practices in detail. Complete the audit below. If there are any areas you are not sure about, look them up using your school programme.

- What is the order of introduction of the first 44 phonemes in your school?
- Does your school teach /ng/, /nk/ and /x/ as three phonemes or are these taught as /n/ and /g/, /n/ and /k/ and /k/ and /s/? Either of these alternatives (or a mixture of both) are possible but your school programme will have made a choice that all teachers should know about.
- When are children taught double letter digraphs for /s/, /z/, /f/ and /l/?
- When are children taught letter names in your school? What do you do for children who do not know them?
- How many phonics sessions do children do each week in Reception, Year 1 and Year 2?
- How is the phonics teaching in your school differentiated?
- Where can you find guidance about the phonics teaching in your school?

Knowledge about recommended lesson structures is an important basis for your planning. Johnson and Watson (2007) have a great deal to say about this topic and recommend the structure picked up by the Letters and sounds programme. They recommend the following.

- Introduction – where objectives are shared and key items of knowledge, such as alphabet names revised.
- Revision – a quick-fire revision of known graphemes and phonemes. There are lots of ways to use

letter cards, objects and formation activities to enliven this phase.
- **New material** – the teacher introduces new graphemes and phonemes and looks at them in different positions in words. Children pronounce and blend new words using cards, magnetic letters and interactive whiteboards to do this visually and physically as well as aurally and orally. Likewise, children segment words to identify the phonemes.
- **Apply** – the children write new words and sentences using the words they can make and tricky words.
- **Follow-up** – where children search for the new letters or graphemes in words and may practise letter formation or the alphabet song.

This lesson structure requires active, well-paced teaching using plenty of visual, oral and physical stimuli. In this respect an electronic whiteboard programme is very useful as children can see the graphemes in and out of words, hear the phonemes and see blending taking place. With such a programme children are regularly reminded of correct pronunciation and the teacher has a large supply of pre-programmed words to call upon. However, an interactive whiteboard is not interactive at all for most children if the interaction is limited to one child occasionally pressing a button. It is much better for the teacher to operate the whiteboard and engage the children in using magnetic letters, letter or grapheme cards and fans and playing active games such as those recommended in Letters and sounds.

In addition to daily phonics lessons it is very important to use phonics in reading and writing, modelling and supporting phonic spelling and decoding in shared and guided reading and writing. This makes it doubly important for you to think quickly about when and how to do this. For instance, when you ask a child to segment a word, check how you do it: village is NOT /v/ /i/ /l/ /l/ /a/ /g/ /e/ but can be segmented as v l ll age – with the emphasis on the first three phonemes and avoiding the irregular /i/. *Yacht* is a waste of time! You need to think quickly, recognise irregularity and remember to ask children what they already know – not what they don't.

Knowledge of your children and their needs and progress

This is indispensable for successful teaching of phonics. As a teacher, you have to decide when children should begin structured phonics – when are they just on the cusp of phonemic awareness so that they can develop this? Then you have to decide how best to meet the needs of all children. Many teachers use a whole-class approach to the teaching of phonics, or break the class into two or three groups. However, this means that you are teaching a good many children at a time. You have to constantly assess who is learning the intended content and, on the basis of this, adjust pace. If some children are struggling to make progress you need to arrange additional experience, with a teaching assistant (TA), working on computer-based resources with you. All this is based on ongoing assessment and recoding of children's knowledge of grapheme-phoneme correspondences, blending, segmenting and use of these skills in their reading and writing.

A SUMMARY OF **KEY POINTS**

Phonics is an entitlement for all children but is only part of good reading and writing instruction.

> **The Rose review has redefined phonics to include phonological awareness, knowledge of grapheme-phoneme correspondences (GPCs), blending and segmenting skills and sight word recognition. Some programmes also include morphemic knowledge.**

> Schools are currently engaged in taking on a synthetic approach to phonics teaching and this involves managing new programmes.

> Phonological and phonemic awareness is essential if they are to learn phonics.

> The progression in phonic knowledge and skills includes simple GPCs, different representations of phonemes and graphemes and the skills of blending and segmenting first CVC, then more complex words.

> Correct pronunciation of phonemes and a known vocabulary for phonics teaching are essential for staff, children and parents, if phonics teaching is to be effective.

> Knowledge of your school programme and policy is the key to effective use.

> Patterned lesson structures throughout the key stage, help children to build and consolidate their phonics learning and to know what to expect.

> Assessment of progress is the key to supporting all children to make progress in phonics.

Moving on

This chapter has concentrated heavily on the importance of shared knowledge and understanding about phonics and phonics teaching and also on common teaching practices.

For any class teacher it is important to consider how you train new staff (such as teaching assistants), supply teachers and trainees, and parents working in school about your policies and practices and to ensure they have the subject knowledge they need.

If you go into a new class, how can you best find out about this? What resources would you need? Who could you ask for support?

REFERENCES REFERENCES **REFERENCES** REFERENCES **REFERENCES** REFERENCES

DCSF (2007) *The Early Years Foundation Stage*. DCSF. Available online at **www.standards.dfes.gov.uk/eyfs/**

DfES (2006) *Independent review of the teaching of early reading (the Rose review)*. DfES. Available online at **www.standards.dfes.gov.uk/rosereview/finalreport**

DfES/PNS (2007) *Framework for Teaching Literacy and Mathematics*. London: DfES. Available online at **www.standards.dfes.gov.uk/primaryframeworks/literacy/**

Department of Education, Science and Training (DEST) (2004) *Teaching reading: report and recommendations*. Commonwealth of Australia.

Dombey, H (2006) Phonics and English orthography in Lewis, M and Ellis, S (eds) *Phonics: practice, research and policy*. London: Paul Chapman Publishing.

Harrison, C (2004) *Understanding reading development*. London: Sage.

Johnson, R and Watson, J (2005) *The effects of synthetic phonics teaching on reading and spelling achievement*. Scottish Executive Education Dept. Available online at **www.scotland.gov.uk**

Johnson, R and Watson, J (2007) *Teaching synthetic phonics*. Exeter: Learning Matters. This book offers a very detailed view of a successful synthetic phonics programme with plenty of examples and advice about teaching.

Lewis, M and Ellis, S (Eds) (2006) *Phonics: practice, research and policy*. London: Paul Chapman Publishing. This book provides an excellent introduction to the research and practice in the area from a wide range of expert perspectives.

MacCartney, E (2006) Developmental issues: Speaking and phonological awareness, in Lewis, M and Ellis, S (eds) *Phonics: practice, research and policy.* London: Paul Chapman Publishing.

Medwell et al (2007) *Primary English Knowledge and Understanding* 3rd edition. Exeter: Learning Matters.

Medwell et al (2007) *Primary English Teaching Theory and Practice* 3rd edition. Exeter: Learning Matters.

National Reading Panel (NRP) (2000) *Teaching children to read: An evidence based assessment of the scientific research literature on reading and its implications for reading instruction*. Washington DC: National Institute for Child Health and Human Development.

PNS/DfES (2007) *Letters and sounds: notes of guidance for practitioners and teachers*. London: DfES. This is the government sponsored programme for phonics.

Solity, J (2006) Responses to Rose in Lewis, M and Ellis, S (eds) *Phonics: practice, research and policy*. London: Paul Chapman Publishing.

Torgerson, C, Brooks, G, and Hall, J, (2006) A systematic review of the research literature on the use of phonics in reading and spelling. *Research Report, 711*. London: DfES. Available online at **www.dfed.gov.uk/research/data/uploadfiles/RR711.pdf**

FURTHER READING FURTHER READING FURTHER READING FURTHER READING

Goswami, U and Bryant, P (1990) *Phonological skills and learning to read*. London: Lawrence Erlbaum

Answers to questions in Practical tasks

Which words contain unknown phonemes? dunk, she bow, chip, egg, get

Which words contain unknown graphemes? bow, chip, pay, egg, get, she, boat, dunk

Which words are not CVC words? flush, blush

Which words contain the split digraph? safe, kite

The alphabet contains 26 **letters**. In spoken English there are around 44 phonemes, depending on your **accent**.

A phoneme is the smallest unit of **sound** in speech. Each phoneme can be represented by one or more **letters**. A grapheme may have one or more **letters**. Graphemes with two letters are called **digraphs**. Graphemes with three letters are trigraphs. Each grapheme can represent one or more **phonemes**.

There are two main types of **phonemes** consonants and vowels. The **20** or so consonants are made by impeding the flow of air through the mouth and nose with the lips, tongue, teeth and palate. Vowels are generally divided into short and **long** vowel phonemes.

Early phonics teaching focuses on consonant, **vowel**, **consonant** words, then moves on to more complicated structures including consecutive **consonants**. Eventually, alternative **graphemes** for each phoneme are learnt and alternative phonemes for each grapheme.

If you have any difficulty with these basic terms, you might want to consult *Primary English: teaching theory and practice*.

3
English vocabulary and the development of language

Chapter objectives

By the end of this chapter you should have developed your understanding of:

- **the history of English vocabulary;**
- **the mechanisms of language change and development;**
- **ways of focusing on vocabulary with your class.**

Professional Standards for QTS:

Q14

Introduction

Words are endlessly fascinating to learners of language (and that means all of us) and the study of words and their origins can be a significant way into enhancing children's appreciation of the subtleties of the English language as a medium for expressing meaning. As an example of this, one of the few lessons I can actually remember from my own primary school experience was taken by a visiting teacher and began by our discussing the word *tomato*. We were asked to spell the plural of that word, *tomatoes*, and then to think of any other words we could which ended in –o. I suggested *piano* and was then asked to spell the plural of that, *pianos*. We discovered that some words which ended in –o made their plurals by adding –es, and that some only added –s. The teacher asked us if we could see any pattern in this and 30 minutes or so of lively group discussion ensued. For the time (1960) this was very enlightened and progressive teaching. We had been used previously to being told the rules about language and spelling, not trying to discover them for ourselves.

My memories of what we decided the rules were are, I admit, only hazy, although I do remember our conclusion that if a word was a short form, it only added an –s. Thus *photos* and *pianos* because these are short for *photographs* and *pianofortes* (not many children today would actually know that). Nowadays I might add to that list *demos*, *memos* and *pros*. Words which were not shortened forms, like *tomatoes* and *potatoes*, added –es.

I have thought further about this since and have realised that another class of o-ending words which add only an –s are those which have been imported into English from another language: *stilettos*, *cellos*, *nintendos*, *chinos* and *avocados*, although there are exceptions to this, e.g. *mangoes*.

The big advantage that is open to us today when we investigate language in this way is that we now have access to electronic word-searching devices, which make such investigations possible without a great deal of fairly random hunting in dictionaries. When looking at the o-ending words problem, for example, it would be useful to get children searching the online British National Corpus (BNC) of language usage. Type 'zeros' into the search box of **http://sara.natcorp.ox.ac.uk/lookup.html**. This should produce 132 examples of this spelling being used (although this free version of the BNC will only show you 50 of these.) Next try 'zeroes' and see the difference. This exercise suggests that one spelling is more normal, even though the other is sometimes used.

PRACTICAL TASK PRACTICAL TASK **PRACTICAL TASK** PRACTICAL TASK **PRACTICAL TASK**

Try the exercise with other o-ending words. Other websites which would be useful for investigations into the origins of words include:
www.wordwizard.com/
www.westegg.com/etymology/
www.askoxford.com/asktheexperts/faq/aboutwordorigins/

Language changes

In the fourteenth century a book in English, called the *Polychronicon*, describes how the Emperor Charlemagne spent ten whole years building a wooden bridge over the Rhine. But one day, shortly before Charlemagne's death, the bridge was destroyed by a fire so powerful that within three hours, 'nought oon spone' was to be seen floating above water. 'Not one spoon'? This is not a story about floating cutlery. At that time, 'spoon' just meant a thin piece of wood, a chip, or a splinter.

Initially, it seems odd that the meaning of 'spoon' has managed to change so much over a relatively short period of time. What is more, such changes in meaning may appear alien to the very purpose of language, which surely is to provide a stable system of conventions that allow communication between members of a society. For how can speakers reliably convey their thoughts to one another if the sense of the words they use can change so rapidly and, comparatively, suddenly? It may therefore come as a surprise that the leap in meaning that 'spoon' has managed over 600 years is by no means unique. When you inspect the history of a language – any language – you quickly discover that change is not the exception but the rule. How does such change happen? And why?

Let us begin by looking at the changes in one supposedly immutable document – the Bible. Here is a short excerpt from the Book of Genesis, which relates the story of the Flood:

English around 2000

The Lord regretted having made humankind on the earth … So the Lord said: 'I will wipe the human beings I have created off the face of the earth, people together with animals and reptiles and birds of the air, because I regret having made them.

And God said to Noah, 'Make yourself an ark of gopher wood … and cover it inside and out with pitch. For my part, I am going to bring a flood of waters on the earth, to destroy all flesh in which there is the breath of life.'

From modern, albeit literary English, we will now jump four centuries back in time, to the year 1604, when King James I, newly installed on the throne of England, and trying to calm the religious strife that had plagued the country for more than a century, commissioned the best scholars in the land to produce a translation of the Bible into the English of the day.

Seven years later, in 1611, what has come to be known as the King James Version was published:

English around 1600 (King James Version)

It repented the Lord that he had made man on the earth ... And the Lord said: 'I will destroy man whom I haue created from the face of the earth, both man, and beast, and the creeping thing, and the foules of the aire, for it repenteth me that I haue made them.'

And God said vnto Noah: 'Make thee an arke of gopher wood ... and [thou] shalt pitch it within and without with pitch. And behold, I, euen I, doe bring a flood of waters vpon the earth, to destroy all flesh wherein is the breath of life.'

Because of the prestige of the King James Version, which is still in use even today, this language seems quite familiar to us (although some of the spelling and transcription might give us pause). But if we venture further back in time, to two centuries before King James commissioned his Bible, things get a little harder. The first translation of the entire Bible into English was undertaken towards the end of the fourteenth century by a group led by John Wycliffe, a forerunner of the Protestant Reformation who challenged the authority of the Church. Wycliffe and his associates worked on making the Bible available to everyone who could read – a bold undertaking for the time. Their translation finally appeared around 1390:

English around 1400 (Wycliffe Bible)

It forthou3t him that he had made man in erthe. 'I shal do awey,' he seith, 'man, whom I made of nou3t, fro the face of the erthe, fro man vnto thingis hauynge soule, fro crepynge beest vnto fowles of heuen; forsothe it othenkith me to haue maad hem.'

He seide to Noe: 'Make to thee an ark of planed trees; and with ynne and with oute thow shal di3ten it with glew. Se, I shal lede to watres of a flood vpon the erthe, and I shal slee al flehs in the which spiryt of lijf is.'

(The symbol 3 corresponds to 'gh' in modern orthography. Thus 'forthou3t' would nowadays be written 'forthought'. The 3 was pronounced with the sound of 'ch' as in Scottish 'loch' but, when printing became standardised, it was often represented by the letter 'z'. This, incidentally, is the explanation for the odd, to modern English ears, pronunciation of the first name of Menzies Campbell, former leader of the Liberal Democrat political party.)

Wycliffe's may have been the first complete Bible to appear in English, but some parts of the Bible had been put into English as early as four centuries earlier. One of the first English translations was made at the turn of the first millennium, by Ælfric, Abbot of Eynsham. Ælfric was celebrated as the greatest prose writer of Anglo-Saxon England, but for speakers of modern English, his language might seem a little odd:

English around 1000 (Translation of Ælfric)

Gode ofðuhte ða ðæt he mann geworhte ofer eorðan ... And cwæð: 'Ic adylgie ðone man, ðe ic gesceop, fram ðære eorðan ansyne, fram ðam men oð ða nytenu, fram ðam slincendum oð ða fugelas: me ofðingð soðlice ðæt ic hi worhte.'

And God cwæð ða to Noe: 'Wyrc ðe nu ane arc of aheawenum bordum and clæmst wiðinnan and wiðutan mid tyrwan. Efne ic gebringe flodes wæteru ofer eorðan, ðæt ic ofslea eal flæsc on ðam ðe is lifes gast.'

(The symbol ð corresponds to 'th' in modern orthography. Thus 'ðæt' corresponds to modern 'that'.)

The four passages above reveal the waywardness of the 'English language' over the last 1000 years, and highlight just how thoroughly it has changed. Within the space of only about 30 generations, 'English' has undergone such a thorough overhaul that what is supposed to be one and the same language is barely recognisable. Indeed, Ælfric's language seems so entirely foreign that we might need some convincing to accept that it even has anything to do with English at all. And yet, on closer inspection, and with a word-for-word comparison with modern English, it turns out that the two 'Englishes' have a lot more in common than meets the eye, as tabulated below.

Gode	ofthuhte	tha	thæt	he	mann	geworhte	ofer	eorthan			
To God	displeased	then	that	he	man	wrought	over	earth			
And	cwæth:	Ic	adylgie	thone	man	the	ic	gesceop	fram	thære	eorthan	ansyne
and	said	I	destroy	the	man	that	I	shaped	from	the	earth's	face
fram	tham	men	oth	tha	nytenu	fram	tham	slincendum	oth	tha	fugelas
from	the	men	to	the	beasts	from	the	crawlers	to	the	fowls

Armed with this, it may become easier to accept that Ælfric's language and modern English really do represent two stages of the same language. Quite a few words are the same (and, he, men), and others are much of a muchness (*ofer* 'over'; *fram* 'from') or at least close enough to be identifiable: *eorthan*, 'earth'; *geworhte*, 'wrought'; *cwæth*, 'quoth'; *fugelas*, 'fowls'. Even so, the knowledge that Ælfric's language really was the 'English' of a millennium ago only makes the extent of the changes seem more baffling.

Perhaps the most surprising feature of Ælfric's English is that, like Latin, it had a complex case and gender system, so that nouns and even the definite article *the* had an array of different forms depending on their role in the sentence and on their gender and number. Just consider how many different forms the article *the* could assume even in the three short lines from the biblical passage above: *thone man* ('the man'), *fram thære eorthan ansyne* ('from the earth's face'), *fram tham men* ('from the men'), *oth tha nytenu* ('to the animals'). To give an idea of the labyrinth of different forms in the English of Ælfric's day, the set of endings for one class of nouns is shown below.

Singular		**Plural**	
thæt wæter	'the water'	*tha wæteru*	'the waters'
tham wætere	'to the water'	*tham wæterum*	'to the waters'
thæs wævteres	'of the water'	*thara wætera*	'of the waters'

It is the case system, perhaps more than anything else, that makes Ælfric's language appear so outlandish, whereas Wycliffe's English seems much less peculiar, largely because by 1400 the case system had almost entirely disappeared. But while the collapse of the case system was an enormous upheaval in the history of English, it was by no means the only change. We only need compare a short phrase from the four passages to appreciate that no area of English stood still for very long.

1000:	me ofthingth sothlice þæt ic hi worhte
1400:	forsothe it othenkith me to haue maad hem
1600:	for it repenteth me that I haue made them
2000:	because I regret having made them

The first thing we notice is how words come and go over the centuries, with older words (like *worhte* 'wrought') dying out, and being replaced by new ones (*maad*). Expressing displeasure, for example, seems to have changed completely. Ælfric uses a verb current at the time, and says *me ofthingth* ('it displeases me'), but by 1400 the verb *ofthink* had begun to sound rather dated. Wycliffe could still expect his readers to understand *it othenkith me*, but by 1600 this verb had long been forgotten, and *it repenteth me* was used in its stead. Today, the verb 'repent' is still easily recognisable, but it nevertheless seems quite out of place here. Since the seventeenth century, 'repent' has undergone a complete role reversal: what the King James translators understood by *it repenteth me* is what we would render with 'I repent (or regret) it'.

CASE STUDY CASE STUDY CASE STUDY CASE STUDY CASE STUDY CASE STUDY

Fair: complexion or beautiful

One class of Year 5 children researched the history of the word *fair*. They understood this to mean 'of light complexion' but understood that at some point it was also used to mean 'beautiful'. They found out that the earliest meaning of the English word *fair* was 'beautiful' or 'pleasing to the eye'. The word in this sense was first recorded in about 888 in King Alfred the Great's translation of the works of Boethius. The English spoken at that time is known as Old English, and *fair* took the form *fæger*. It derives from the Old Teutonic root *fagro*. Surprisingly, the *fair* which means 'free from bias, fraud, or injustice' comes from this same root, which in turn derives from an Indo-European root fag – with a meaning of 'fitting' or 'suitable'.

Fair with the meaning 'beautiful' is no longer used today, except in literature, and even then it is considered somewhat old-fashioned. Shakespeare, Milton and Dryden all used it poetically in this sense. The 'complexion' sense of fair does not appear in the written record until 1551. This meaning simply developed from the notion that women of light complexion were considered beautiful, as light skin meant a woman was not working outside, the fate of the lower classes. The 'beautiful' meaning of *fair* was applied to women who had light skin, as they were considered beautiful, and the 'light-skin' meaning slowly replaced the 'beautiful' meaning.

The children were intrigued at this because they were more used to tanned people being considered beautiful. After some research (the website **www.skincarederm.com/history.htm** was very useful) they discovered that tans did not become fashionable until the 1920s when Coco Chanel, the fashion designer, accidentally acquired a tanned skin during a yachting holiday.

But it is not just the meaning of words that changes over time. Some of the basic features in the structure of English, such as the conventions of word order, also seem to have been rather unstable. Word order, for example, plays a crucial role in modern English, as it is the only means of distinguishing the subject (which comes before the verb) from the object (which comes after). But consider the order of words in Ælfric's passage: *me ofthingth* – 'me displeases' (for 'it displeases me'), and *ic hi worhte* – 'I them made' (for 'I made them'). Clearly, Ælfric's idea of which words should go where was different to ours.

Finally, the pronunciation of English words has also strayed considerably over the centuries, but these changes can only partially be seen in the passages above, because of the conservative nature of the writing system. Only in a few cases, such as the word *ic* in Ælfric's passage, can the changes in pronunciation be glimpsed from the spelling. *Ic* is in fact one and the same word as our modern 'I', and only looks so different because its pronunciation has changed so much. In the tenth century, *ic* was pronounced something like {itch}, but by 1400 the final {tch) had disappeared, and the word came to be pronounced {ee} (as in 'bee'), and thus to be spelt as just 'I'. In the writing system, 'I' has looked the same ever since, but the actual pronunciation of 'I' has continued to develop. During the fifteenth century, there was an upheaval in the pronunciation of many English vowels, which linguists call 'the Great English vowel shift'. As a part of this shift, all long {ee} vowels turned into {ay} (as in modern 'day'), so by the sixteenth century, 'I' came to be pronounced {ay}. And by the eighteenth century, {ay} changed further into the modern pronunciation {eye}.

Most of the changes in pronunciation, however, are masked by the spelling. For cultural reasons, the system of spelling we use today has remained pretty much frozen for at least 400 years, even though the pronunciation has continued to drift during this time. So if we compare the King James passage with the modern translation, we can easily be misled into thinking that changes in pronunciation came to a halt after 1611. But this is an illusion. Take, for instance, the phrase 'flood of waters to destroy all flesh'. The King James translators spelt this phrase just as we do. But in fact, most of the words in this phrase would have sounded quite different then. In 1611, the word *flood* rhymed with *good*; *waters* had an audible {r}, and was pronounced roughly with the vowels of modern {matters}; and the word *all* sounded like our word {owl}.

The frozen spelling system also conceals changes in pronunciation that occurred even more recently. When reading Jane Austen or George Eliot, for example, we are tempted to assume that their characters sounded just like the actors in a BBC television version. In 1902, however, the art critic Charles Eastlake reminisced about the speech of 'old fellows' 40 years before, those people born around 1800, who would have been in their teens when Jane Austen's novels first appeared.

> *Men of mature age can remember many words which in the conversation of old fellows forty years ago would sound strangely to modern ears. They were generally much obleeged for a favour. They referred affectionately to their darters; talked of goold watches, or of a recent visit to Room; mentioned that they had seen the Dook of Wellington in Hyde Park last Toosday and that he was in the habit of rising at sivin o'clock. They spoke of Muntague Square and St Tummus's 'Ospital. They would profess themselves to be their hostess's 'umble servants, and to admire her collection of chayney, especially the vase of Prooshian blue.*

So although the conventions of spelling might not have changed much for nearly four centuries, pronunciation certainly has. And it is for this reason that English spelling is so infamously irrational. It is actually unfair to say that English spelling is not an accurate rendering of speech. It is – but it renders the speech of the sixteenth century.

It is clear, then, that no aspect of the English language has remained protected from changes: sounds, meanings and structures all seem to be unable to stay still. This is not just true of English – all languages change, all the time. The only static languages are dead ones.

This linguistic diversity is a direct consequence of the geographical dispersal of populations, and language's own propensity to change. The idea that there was originally one single primitive human language is not impossible, but even if it were true, it was very early in human prehistory that different groups started splitting up, going their own ways and settling across the globe, changing their languages in different ways. So the huge diversity of languages in the world today simply reflects how long languages have had to change independently of one another.

Obviously some languages are much more closely related than others. English, for instance, is more similar to Swedish, Icelandic, Dutch and German than it is to Polish, Albanian, Punjabi, Persian, Turkish, Yoruba (spoken in Nigeria) or Chinese, as can be seen below.

English: Give us this day our daily bread
Swedish: Giv oss i dag vart dagliga brod
Icelandic: Gef oss i dag vort daglegt brauð
Dutch: Geef ons heden ons dagelijks brood
German: Gib uns heute unser tagliches Brot

Polish: Chleba naszego powszedniego daj nam dzisiaj
Albanian: Buken tone te perditeshme jepna neve sot
Punjabi: Sadi gujar jogi roti aj sanun dih
Persian: Nan-e-ruane-ye-mara dar in ruz be-ma bebakhs
Turkish: Bugun bize giindelik ekmegimizi ver
Chinese: Women riyong de yinshi jinri cigei women
Yoruba: Fun wa li onje ojo wa loni

The reason why English, Dutch, German and the Scandinavian languages look so alike is that they all stem from one prehistoric ancestor, which linguists call Proto-Germanic, so in fact they were all one and the same language until the beginning of the first millennium AD. But once the Germanic tribes started spreading out from their original homelands in southern Scandinavia and along the North Sea and Baltic coasts, their speech varieties gradually began to diverge, eventually turning into different languages.

English and the Germanic languages are themselves related, more distantly, to many other languages of Europe and Asia. Ultimately, they go back to the same common ancestor as that of Italian, French, Spanish, Irish, Welsh, Russian, Lithuanian, Polish, Greek, Albanian, and even Armenian, Persian, Hindi and Punjabi. This ancestral prehistoric tongue, probably spoken around 6,000 years ago, is called by linguists Proto-Indo-European, because in the first few millennia BC the descendants of its speakers spread over an area stretching all the way from India to Europe. So although it may not be immediately apparent to the naked eye, the second group of languages in the list above (Polish, Albanian, Punjabi and Persian) are all related to English, albeit somewhat distantly, and are descended from the same original tongue. But since English and Persian, for instance, must have parted company at least six millennia ago, the two languages have diverged so much that only a few basic Persian words are still immediately identifiable (for instance *pedar*, 'father'; *dokhtar*, 'daughter'; or *do*, 'two'). So to the naked eye, the Persian or Albanian sentences above do not look much more similar to English than the ones from Turkish or Yoruba, which are not descended from Proto-Indo-European.

CASE STUDY CASE STUDY CASE STUDY CASE STUDY CASE STUDY CASE STUDY

Teeth and dentistry

One class of Year 6 children became intrigued as to why the person who looked after their teeth was not called a 'toothist' but a 'dentist'. They were surprised to find (from **www.answers.com/topic/tooth**) that the word 'tooth' is in fact a linguistic cousin of *dental*, *dentist* and *dandelion*. The source of all these words is the Indo-European root word *dent–*, 'tooth', which ultimately derives from another root, *ed–*, meaning 'to bite', the ancestor of our *eat*. In some languages the pronunciation of *dent–* drifted through *dont–* to the ancient Germanic *tanthuz*. The Anglo-Saxons dropped the *n*, giving us the Old English *toth* which we now write as *tooth*. Another Germanic derivative of *dent–* was *tunthsk*, which in Old English became *tusc*, 'a canine tooth' and ancestor of *tusk*.

The root word *dent–* is clearly seen in French *dent*, 'tooth', but it is not so apparent in *dandelion*. This familiar weed takes its name from deep serrations in its leaves which, to some, looked like a lion's tooth – *dent de lion* in French. The children were also excited to learn that the word for *dandelion* in French is actually *pissenlit* (**en.wikipedia.org/wiki/Dandelion**), which refers more to the effects of eating this plant that to what it looks like!

Why do languages change?

Change, as we have seen, is a fundamental characteristic of all languages. This fact does not, however, answer the fundamental question of why. Why are languages constantly changing, and how does this change happen?

One obvious explanation is that change is not simply characteristic of language. The world around us is changing all the time, and naturally, language has to change with it. Language needs to keep pace with new realities, new technologies and new ideas, from ploughs to laser printers, and from political correctness to SMS-texting, and that is why it always changes. This line of argument seems appealing at first, but when one looks at the actual changes close up, the picture becomes far more complicated. Take, for instance, this short phrase from the passages quoted earlier:

AD 1000:   me ofthingth sothlice þæt ic hi worhte
AD 2000:   I regret having made them

What new inventions or new ideas could have been behind the differences here? Which new technology, for example, could have sparked the change in sounds from *ic* {itch} to *I* {eye}? And which new invention is responsible for the switch in the order of the words, from 'them made' (*hi worhte*) to 'made them'? This suggests that our first 'obvious' explanation for why language keeps on changing is not actually that convincing. Even if some changes in language come about in order to adapt to changing realities, these constitute only a minor part of the overall transformations that languages undergo. Most changes come about for different reasons.

A second 'obvious' explanation for why language changes so much is that it is to do with contact. Languages might change simply because their speakers come into contact with speakers of other languages or dialects, and start borrowing words and expressions from one another. This explanation is specially tempting in the case of English, since although English is a Germanic language, about half of its vocabulary is not of Germanic origin but borrowed from various other languages, mostly Norman French and Latin. But while contact is undoubtedly the source of a great many changes, it still cannot be held responsible for the sweeping changes in absolutely all languages, even those whose speakers have had hardly any exposure to other languages. And what's more, even in the case of English, many of the changes, for example, from *ic* {itch } to {ee} to {ay} to {eye}, cannot just be put down to borrowing.

These 'obvious' explanations account for only some of the changes in language. Of more fundamental importance, perhaps, are other processes which produce an accumulation of unintended small-scale actions. These can be described as economy, expressiveness and analogy.

Economising with language

Economy refers to the tendency to save effort, and is behind the short-cuts speakers often take in pronunciation. When these short-cuts accumulate, they can create new sounds, and new words. As an example of this, take the Old English term *hlaf-weard*, literally 'loaf warden' or 'bread guard' (*w–* and *gu–* are common shifts between languages: for example, the English *William* links to the French *Guillaume*). This was shortened to *hlaford* then *laferd*, *lowerd*, and finally *lord*.

Economising like this has often had the effect of making the final parts of words redundant, as if speakers could not be bothered to pronounce the whole word once it was clear to the listener what they were going to say. For example, in modern English words like *loved* and *disturbed* are written with *–ed* at the end but pronounced {lovd} and {disturbd}. This used not to be the case and before 1700 or so the usual pronunciation was to include the 'ed'. In poetry of the eighteenth century (and even occasionally earlier, such as in Shakespeare's work) the distinction in pronunciation would often be indicated by writing these words either *lov'd* or *lovèd*, or *disturb'd* or *disturbèd*. Nowadays, to make such a distinction seems archaic and the shortened pronunciation has more or less taken over entirely.

Such economising in pronunciation can readily be seen in modern language. There can hardly be a speaker of English who pronounces fully the sentence 'I do not know', 'I don't know' being very common, or even '(I) dunno'. The same process can be seen in French, with 'je ne sais pas' being almost universally pronounced as {shepa}. This process causes controversy when pronunciation begins to affect spelling. The French are long past worrying about the shortening of 'Cela va' to 'Ça va' and they even now regularly write 'Ça va pas' for the negative ('Cela ne vas pas' would be the original). In English, there is still a resistance to many such shortenings, with even common abbreviations such as 'don't' being discouraged in writing (it is impossible to discourage them in speech, so well established are they).

An interesting example of this shortening beginning the long road to acceptability concerns the *have* in verb forms such as 'should have' or 'would have'. These are usually pronounced 'should've' or 'would've', with the final phoneme sounding exactly like the normal pronunciation of the word *of*. Not surprisingly, many young children write these as 'should of' and 'would of' because that is what they sound like. More surprising, however, is the fact that a Google search on 'should of' gives 1,390,000 web pages where this construction appears. I have not checked all of these (obviously!) but, of the first 50, only about ten were pages where some discussion of the usage appeared. On the rest, 'should of' appears as if it were the normal way of writing such an expression. This is evidence, surely, of the normalisation of this way of writing this expression and gives us an example of language change in process.

Expressiveness in language

Expressiveness relates to speakers' attempts to achieve greater effect for their utterances and extend their range of meaning. One area where we are particularly expressive is in saying 'no'. A plain 'no' is often deemed too weak to convey the depth of our unenthusiasm, so to make sure the right effect is achieved, we beef up 'no' to 'not at all', 'not a bit', 'no way', 'by no means', 'not in a million years', and so on. Of course, once phrases like these become the established way of expressive the negative, their currency begins to be devalued and language users seek for other ways of expressing the idea more forcefully. And so the language develops, continually adding new possibilities for expression.

New words are constantly being added to the English language, and, indeed, always have been. New words are not totally new. The vast majority are made up out of existing components. The same word-formation processes recur around the globe, though each language has its own particular favourites.

Compounds

In English, compounding has been the most prolific process throughout the twentieth century. It consists simply of putting words together. Sometimes these remain as two words. Recent examples include *airport fiction* (books, especially ones that are not very serious, that people buy at airports to read while they are travelling on planes) and *hot desk* (a desk which is used by different workers on different days, instead of by the same worker every day). At other times, the two parts are joined into a single new word, for example *jobseeker* (someone who is trying to find a job), and *webhead* (someone who uses the internet a lot, especially in a skilful way). Sometimes the two parts are linked by a hyphen, as in *walk-in*, a recent adjective that describes a place to which you can go without an appointment, as in *walk-in clinic*.

Affixes

Affixation is another common method of forming new words. An affix is an additional part of a word added at the beginning (prefix) or end of the word (suffix). Adding an ending to an existing word continues to produce many new words in English. For example, *–iac* has been added to the word *brain* to created the recent new word *brainiac* (someone who spends a lot of time studying and thinking about complicated ideas, but who is often unable to communicate with people in ordinary social situations: 'Electrical engineering is the perfect career for a brainiac like him'). This word is also used as an adjective: 'The company is trying to change its brainiac image'.

Many new words have also been created through the addition of the suffix *–isation*, as in *dollarisation* (a situation in which countries outside the US want to use the dollar rather than their own country's money) or *globalisation* (the process by which countries all over the world become connected, especially because large companies are doing business in many different countries). This is, in fact, two suffixes combined, *–ise* as in *globalise*, then with an added *–ation*.

Another increasingly popular suffix is *–land*, as in *adland* (the activity or business of advertising, considered as a whole: 'Anything that grabs your attention is good in adland') and *cyberland* (activity that involves the internet and the people who use it).

Prefixes have become more widespread recently. *Cyber–* is a good example of a prefix which has been used to create a range of new words (originally meaning 'computer', now often meaning 'to do with the internet'). For example *cybercafé, cybercrime, cyberfraud* (the illegal act of deceiving people on the internet in order to gain money, power, etc.). And dozens of new words formed by prefixes relate to size, both large size and very small size, such as *micro–, super–,* and *multi–*, as in the following.

- **Microbrewery, a small company that makes only a small quantities of beer, and often has a restaurant where its beer is served.**
- **Microengineering, the activity of designing structures and machines that are extremely small.**
- **Micromanage, to organise and control all the details of other people's work in a way that they find annoying.**
- **Supersize, a supersize drink or meal in a fast-food restaurant is the largest size that the restaurant serves.**
- **Multi-tasking, a computer's ability to do more than one job at a time or a person's ability to do the same.**

These prefixes mostly have clear meanings. But suffixes too may have meanings: *–ism* is a suffix which has acquired a more specific meaning in recent years, alongside *–ist*. At one time, its meaning was fairly neutral, as in *pacifism* (the belief that all wars and all forms of violence are wrong). But gradually *–ism* has taken on a feeling of disapproval: *ageism* is unfair treatment of people because they are old, and someone who is prejudiced in this way is an *ageist*. Similarly, *lookist* is unfairly deciding to like or not like someone by considering only the way they look, their weight, their clothes, etc. The *–ism* is *lookism*, and the person who discriminates is a *lookist*. (I was once warned at an in-service teachers' course not to be 'darrenist', that is, to be prejudiced against a child simply because his name happened to be Darren!)

Conversion (change of word class)
Conversion, the change of a word from one word class (part of speech) to another, is very common in today's English. It is easy for a language with few word endings to use this process, as with to *bookmark* (a verb formed from a noun) meaning to save the address of a page on the internet, so that you can find it again easily; to *ramp* or to *ramp something up* (a verb formed from a noun), meaning to try to persuade people that a company's shares are worth more than they really are; and to *sample* (a verb formed from a noun) is to use a small part of a song from a CD or record in a new song.

Acronyms and abbreviations
Acronyms, initial letters of words, have been important for some time, and abbreviations such as *RIP* ('rest in peace', used on tombstones and in speech about someone who is dead) and *asap* ('as soon as possible') are widely known and used. Some of these acronyms become accepted as full words, such as *laser* ('light amplification by the stimulated emission of radiation', meaning a device that can emit an intense beam of light), which is pronounced as a word. Recently, acronyms and abbreviations have grown increasingly frequent, at least among teenagers and young adults, partly because of mobile phones, or cell phones, which can also send text messages, but which have very limited space on their screens. So brief

message abbreviations are becoming common, such as IMHO ('in my humble opinion') and CUL ('see you later'), though caution is needed. Some abbreviations are ambiguous: LOL could mean either 'lots of love' or 'laughing out loud'!

Blends

Two words combined into one are known as blends. A few blends have become an accepted part of English, such as *brunch*, a mixture of breakfast and lunch, and some of them are intentionally humorous. Here are some examples.

- *Netizen*, someone who uses the internet, especially someone who uses it in a responsible way. This word comes from a combination of the words 'net', meaning 'the internet', and 'citizen'.
- *Netiquette*, the commonly accepted rules for polite behaviour when communicating with other people on the internet: netiquette says that you don't use all capital letters in an e-mail, because that shows you are angry.
- The word *imagineer*, from 'imagination' and 'engineer', means someone who has a lot of new ideas, and who is also able to use these ideas to do practical things.

Analogy in language

The third motive for change, analogy, is shorthand for the mind's craving for order, the instinctive need of speakers to find regularity in language. The effects of analogy are most conspicuous in the errors of young children, as in 'I goed' or 'two foots', which are simply attempts to introduce regularity to areas of the language that happen to be quite disorganised. Many such 'errors' are corrected as children grow up, but some innovations do catch on. In the past, for example, there were many more irregular plural nouns in English: one *boc* (book), many *bec*; one *hand*, two *hend*; one *eye*, two *eyn*; one *cow*, many *kine*. But gradually, 'errors' like *hands* crept in by analogy on the regular *–s* plural pattern. So *bec* was replaced by the 'incorrect' *bokes* (books) during the thirteenth century, *eyn* was replaced by *eyes* in the fourteenth century, *kine* by *cows* in the sixteenth.

REFLECTIVE TASK
REFLECTIVE TASK

Try thinking of some examples of your own which illustrate changes in language use. See the 'Moving on' section below for a further activity which you can undertake with children.

A SUMMARY OF **KEY POINTS**

In this chapter we have:

> explored the concept of language change, particularly related to the ways in which English has changed over the past 1000 years;
> examined some of the mechanisms of language change;
> suggested some starting points for investigations into language which you might use with your pupils.

Moving on

The most important point arising from this chapter is that language is in a perpetual state of change. While no one in particular seems to be trying to change it, a few deep-rooted motives that drive all of us (economy, expressiveness, analogy) create powerful forces of change and ensure that sounds, meanings and structures are always on the move. And while our capacity to accommodate variation means that we are often hardly aware that one form is usurping another, changes can proceed so quickly that after just a few centuries a language can bear little resemblance to its previous form.

One very useful activity you can engage in with a group of learners is to speculate on the ways in which change might continue to happen in the English language. Ask them to think about words they commonly use that their parents might not use so frequently, or use differently. You can start with the obvious, such as *regular* or *wicked*, which mean completely different things now than they did 15 to 20 years ago (if you asked for 'a regular coffee', would you expect one every hour, or a medium-sized one?) You might then progress onto more extreme examples, such as the following.

- **Beast** – an adjective to describe something that's really cool.
- **Book** – cool. The first option given in predictive text when trying to type c-o-o-l.
- **Clappin'** – out of date or worn out, usually to describe attire or accessories, as in 'man, my tracksuit is clappin'. Gotta get down JJB Sport and buy a new one.' Also means tired out.
- **Dry** – dull, boring, stupid, unfunny. A bad joke might be described as 'dry'.
- **Munter** – ugly. An alternative to *minger*, which has long since passed into the mainstream since its first recorded use in 1995.
- **Owned** – to be made a fool of, to be beaten by. Can also be spelled 'pwned', to denote a common spelling error in online gaming slang.
- **Rinsed** – overused, used up, all gone. 'That song was rinsed, I don't like it anymore.'

Explore, either with your pupils or by yourself, the Word Spy web site (**www.wordspy.com**), which contains some amazing examples of new words in English.

FURTHER READING FURTHER READING FURTHER READING FURTHER READING

In pursuing the ideas touched upon in this chapter, there is probably only one author whose works you simply have to read, and that is David Crystal, whose many books on the subject of language are, as well as rigorous and academically sound, all extremely well written and easy to read. Try the following as starters:

Crystal, D (1995) *The Cambridge encyclopaedia of the English language*. Cambridge: Cambridge University Press

Crystal, D (2001) *Language and the internet*. Cambridge: Cambridge University Press

Crystal, D (2006) *Words, words, words*. Oxford: Oxford University Press

4
Looking closely at spelling

Chapter objectives

By the end of this chapter you should have developed your understanding of:

- **some of the problems of English spelling;**
- **some strategies for remembering the spelling of particular kinds of words;**
- **some ways of investigating spelling with your class.**

Professional Standards for QTS

Q14

Introduction

Our Strange Lingo

When the English tongue we speak.
Why is break not rhymed with freak?
Will you tell me why it's true
We say sew but likewise few?
And the maker of the verse,
Cannot rhyme his horse with worse?
Beard is not the same as heard
Cord is different from word.
Cow is cow but low is low
Shoe is never rhymed with foe.
Think of hose, dose, and lose
And think of goose and yet with choose
Think of comb, tomb and bomb,
Doll and roll or home and some.
Since pay is rhymed with say
Why not paid with said I pray?
Think of blood, food and good.
Mould is not pronounced like could.
Wherefore done, but gone and lone –
Is there any reason known?
To sum up all, it seems to me
Sound and letters don't agree.

This poem, written by Lord Cromer and published in the *Spectator* on 9 August, 1902, nicely illustrates some of the vagaries of English spelling and English words. The rules governing spelling and word formation in English can appear so perverse that it is a legitimate question to ask whether, in fact, there are any rules. English is a mongrel language, subject to so many different historical influences that it can be hard to detect any clear patterns in the construction of its words. It is little wonder, perhaps, that many of those who have studied, and taught, the English language have fallen back on the rules inherent in a nice, logical language like Latin to describe, and prescribe, what is permissible and acceptable in English. Of course, this attempt has always missed the point. Latin is not a living language; nobody speaks it any more and therefore it is not developing in response to a host of outside influences, as English is. The responsiveness of English to these influences, from Celtic, through Norman French and Old Norse, to American and European inputs today, and its willingness to adapt and take on new words, new spellings and new language structures, is in fact the secret of its success. English is the global language precisely because of this adaptability.

Nevertheless, as a teacher you will need to think carefully about how you try to make sense of the English word and spelling system for your pupils. It is the aim of this chapter and the next to introduce a number of strategies for doing just that and to try to give you some understanding of how English words come to be written as they are. This understanding will lead to more effective spelling on the part of the children you teach (and also, maybe, on your own part). We will begin by looking more closely at some words which are always tricky to spell.

How good is your spelling?

There is probably nobody who has absolutely perfect spelling all the time (although there are several people who act as if they think they do.)

REFLECTIVE TASK

REFLECTIVE TASK

As a test of your own spelling you might like to look at the words in the following table. In each row only one word is spelt correctly. Can you identify which it is?

1)	dessicate	desiccate	desicate
2)	milenium	millenium	millennium
3)	dumbel	dumbbell	dumbell
4)	supercede	supersede	superceed
5)	accidently	acidently	accidentally
6)	minuscule	miniscule	minniscule
7)	coollie	coolly	cooly
8)	accomodate	accommodate	acommodate
9)	iresistible	irresistible	irresistable
10)	harras	harass	harrass
11)	definitely	definately	difinitely
12)	occurrance	occurence	occurrence
13)	embarass	embaras	embarrass
14)	innoculate	inoculate	innockulate
15)	wiered	weird	wierd

In the sections which follow, we will give you the correct spellings for each of these words, and then, where possible, discuss some of the ways we might disentangle the words to make the reasons for this spelling apparent. You can use this information at an appropriate level to help your pupils gain a similar understanding.

1) Desiccate

To work out the spelling of this word (which is perhaps not one you use on a day-to-day basis), you ideally need to know something about Latin word origins and about what is perhaps the most common way of building words in English.

Many English words are built of three components, each of which carries part of the word meaning: a root, preceded by a prefix and followed by a suffix. Thus the word *imported* has the root *port* (meaning *carry*, as in the French word *porter*), with the prefix *im–*, implying a direction of carry, in this case inwards, and the suffix *–ed*, indicating that this action occurred in the past. Such affixing is a very clever system with immense potential for forming new words to meet new situations. One newspaper commentator recently termed the current Iraq conflict as 'a meganation bullying a minination', thus coining two completely new words which his readers nevertheless instantly understood! The affixing system can also be very useful for engaging children with words. Most children love long words. My ten-year-old son has already discovered the joys of *antidisestablishmentarianism*, just as I did when I was his age. We will discuss later some ways in which teachers can build upon such fascination with words.

Looking at our target word, we know that *de–* is a common prefix in English, usually indicating some kind of removal. We *debug* a computer program, removing the bugs, or mistakes. Divers *decompress* before surfacing, removing the pressure on their lungs. *Des–* is not a common prefix, which suggests that we have to break this word up into *de + siccate*. It cannot have a double *s*, since no words begin *ss*.

So what about the second part of the word? How do we know whether it is spelt *siccate* or *sicate*? There are two clues. Firstly, we can apply our knowledge of phonic rules in English. One of these tells us that a vowel followed by a single consonant and then another vowel will usually be long. If this vowel is to be short it has to be followed by a double consonant. Think about the differences between the following pairs of words;

hopping   hoping
matting   mating

So if our word part were spelt *sicate* the *i* would have to be long, as in *line*.

The other, rather more obscure, clue is that this word is derived from the Latin *siccus*, meaning *dry*. There are few remnants left in English of this word (although there are in French, where *sec* means *dry*), but if you do a Google search on the term *hortus siccus*, you will find that gardeners use it to refer to a 'dry (or dried) garden, usually referring to a collection of dried and pressed plants'. Obscure indeed, but some children will be fascinated by this sort of investigation.

2) Millennium

Here is a word for which knowledge of Latin origins might also help, but in this case simply thinking about what the word means should give a good clue as to its spelling. It means 'a thousand years' and it has two parts, the prefix *mill–*, which means *thousand*, and *–ennium* which means *years*.

There are several words in English which feature the *mill–* prefix: *millimetre* – a thousandth part of a metre, *millipede* – an insect with (supposedly) a thousand legs, *milligram* – a thousandth part of a gram, even *milliners* in its traditional sense of a shop with a thousand things to sell. The key thing is to distinguish this from the word part *mil–*, which occurs in words such as *military* and *militia* and has its origins in the Latin *miles* meaning *soldier*.

For the second part of the word, we might draw a parallel with *annual* or *anno domini* and so be convinced it needs a double *n*. We might also, following our discussion of *desiccate*, note that if the word were spelt *millenium*, it would have to be pronounced with a long central vowel: *'mill – ee – nium'*.

3) Dumbbell

This is a word in which hardly anyone gets the double *b* in the middle, and even when you know this is correct, the word still looks wrong! You can get children to investigate this word and, unless they find it for themselves, you can point them to the online Wikipedia encyclopaedia (**http://en.wikipedia.org/wiki/Dumbbell**) where they will find the following:

> *Dumbbells, as a word, originated in Tudor England – the devices used for ringing church bells were widely known for their impact on increasing muscle size, creating a trend in the 16th Century which saw rich young men installing similar devices in their homes, consisting of a pulley with a weighted rope which the user pulled as though he was ringing a church bell. These were known as 'bells', but as there were no actual bells on the end of the pulling ropes and were silent, they came to be known colloquially as 'dumb-bells'. Over the centuries, the pulley and weighted rope fell out of fashion, leaving just the weight.*

This word neatly illustrates a common trend in English words; that is, they might start as two words (dumb bells), eventually become so closely linked they acquire a hyphen (dumb-bells) and finally even the hyphen disappears (dumbbells). Hyphens in words are, apparently, an endangered species. The 2007 edition of the *Shorter Oxford English Dictionary* includes 16,000 words which once would have contained a hyphen but now no longer do so. In some cases, the formerly hyphenated words are now split in two, as in:

- fig leaf;
- hobby horse;
- ice cream;
- pin money;
- pot belly;
- test tube;
- water bed.

In others, formerly hyphenated words are now unified into one, for example:

- bumblebee;
- chickpea;
- crybaby;
- leapfrog;
- logjam;
- lowlife;
- pigeonhole;
- touchline;
- waterborne.

There will always, however, be a need for hyphens, because occasionally they make a real difference in terms of meaning. Think of the difference between teaching twenty-odd children and teaching twenty odd children. Or think which you would rather encounter – a man-eating shark or a man eating shark?

4) Supersede

Many people will want to spell this word as *supercede*, drawing a parallel with *precede*. It sounds as though these two words ought to have some link. In fact, they have completely different origins. The *–cede* in *precede* comes from the Latin *cedere*, meaning *to go*. With the prefix, the word means *to go before*, and it has parallels in *recede – to go back*, *proceed – to go forward* and *succeed – to go next* (even though the *cede* is spelt differently in these last two). The word *supersede* derives instead from the Latin *supersedere*, meaning *to sit above*, and so is related to words such as *sedentary* and *sedan*. A useful strategy in teaching spelling is to get pupils to build up word families, or webs, such as these for themselves. Figure 4.1 shows a word web based around the root word 'Sign'. Using this with primary pupils might just make some of them aware of why there is a 'g' in 'sign'.

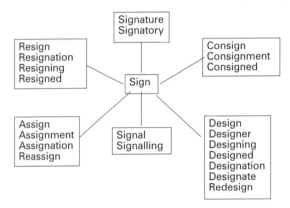

Figure 4.1 A word web around 'sign'

5) Accidentally

Here is an example of a word where, unless we are pedantic, the pronunciation can defeat us when we come to spelling it. Similar problems occur with words such as *incidentally*, *regimentally*, *fundamentally*. We hardly pronounce that final *–al–* so the temptation is to write these words without it.

The crucial knowledge which helps here is grammatical: these words are adverbs – they describe verbs, in the same way that adjectives describe nouns. Adverbs are formed from adjectives in one of the simplest and most productive 'rules' in English: just add *–ly*. Look at these pairs of words:

adjective	**adverb**
quick	quickly
rapid	rapidly
slow	slowly
public	publicly
	accidentally

Now what word will go in the adjective column to match with *accidentally*? A moment's thought tells us it cannot be *accident* – that is a noun, not an adjective. The adjective is *accidental*, which tells us where that *-al* comes from. The same process can be applied with the other words in this family.

adjective	adverb
incidental	incidentally
regimental	regimentally
fundamental	fundamentally

6) Minuscule

Minuscule originally had quite a particular meaning, referring to the smaller form (lower case) of letters (*minuscula littera* in Latin, *minuscula* meaning 'less', as in our word *minus* today). Originally alphabets were written entirely in *majuscule* (capital) letters. When written quickly with a pen, these tended to become rounder and simpler and it is from these that the first minuscule handwriting systems developed. Later it became common to mix both majuscule and minuscule letters in a single text.

The word itself is often spelt *miniscule*, by association with the unrelated word *miniature* and the prefix *mini*. This is traditionally regarded as a spelling mistake, but is now so common that dictionaries tend to accept it as a spelling variation. In *Merriam-Webster's Dictionary of English Usage* (1989), for example, part of the entry 'miniscule, minuscule', notes:

> This spelling [miniscule] was first recorded at the end of the 19th century (minuscule dates back to 1705), but it did not begin to appear frequently in edited prose until the 1940s. Its increasingly common use parallels the increasingly common use of the word itself, especially as an adjective meaning 'very small'.'

During the last half of the twentieth century, dictionaries have been adding *miniscule*. One example is the *Concise Oxford Dictionary*. The eighth edition, published in the mid-1980s, does have an entry for *miniscule*, but labels it as erroneous. However the ninth edition (1995) lists *miniscule* as simply a variant spelling.

Also noted in the 'miniscule, minuscule' entry in *Merriam-Webster's Dictionary of English Usage* is this:

> It may be, in fact, that miniscule is now the more common form. An article by Michael Kenney in the Boston Globe on 12 May 1985 noted that miniscule outnumbered minuscule by three to one in that newspaper's data base.

Incidentally, the term *lower case* comes from manual typesetting. Since minuscules were more frequent in text than majuscules, typesetters often stored them on the lower shelf of a desk to keep them within easy reach.

7) Coolly

This is the only word in the list where you can give yourself a mark however you chose to spell it. All three of these spellings are in current usage, although they do have different meanings.

The word *coolie* has been used in English since the late sixteenth century to refer to hired labourers in India and China. The word probably originated from the Hindi *quli* meaning *hired servant*. Today it has a very archaic feel to it and probably only really exists in the reference to a distinctive circular, pointed hat. Several dictionaries give *cooly* as a variant of this word, which probably results from a simple mistake. One pluralisation rule in English tells us that words ending in -*y* when made plural change that –*y* to –*ies* (*lady* – *ladies*: *baby* – *babies*). So by working backwards from the plural *coolies*, we have developed *cooly* as a possible singular form, although that is not what the word originally was. Mistakes like this are not uncommon in the history of English (they parallel the mistakes made by young children learning English who will often overgeneralise rules to produce words like *foots*, *runned* and *mouses*.)

When we mean *in a cool manner*, we ideally would follow the rules about adverb formation that emerged when we discussed word 5. That is, to form an adverb we simply add –*ly* to an adjective. The adjective is *cool*, so the adverb must be *coolly*, and this would certainly be the normal way to spell this word.

How do we explain, then, that in Dickens' *Oliver Twist* (available at the Project Gutenberg site – **www.gutenberg.org/dirs/etext96/olivr11.txt**) we find the following passage?

> The girl was alone; lying with her head upon the table, and her hair straggling over it. 'She has been drinking,' thought the Jew, cooly, 'or perhaps she is only miserable.'

Of course, this could simply be a mistake, and the word does appear spelt *coolly* elsewhere in the same book. However, the *Free Dictionary* (available at – **www.thefreedictionary.com**) gives several other literary examples of this word being spelt incorrectly, which leaves us rather puzzled.

Probably the best thing to conclude from exploring this particular word is that, actually, spelling is not as certain as we think it should be. It if were, then we could have no words like *picnic*, *tragic*, *magic*, etc. because Dr Johnson in his landmark dictionary of 1755 told us that 'No word ends in -c'.

8) Accommodate

There are some words in which the rules, if there are any which apply, are just too complex to be at all useful in figuring out a spelling. *Accommodate* is one such. Even if we could remember the double *m* by linking the word to *commode*, this would not help us with that double *c*. Perhaps the best thing to do is to fix this one in mind with a mnemonic. Try: 'This word is large enough to accommodate both a double *c* and a double *m.'*

This reminds me of my old biology teacher who used to tell us that 'possess possesses as many s's as it can possess'. That certainly helped me remember the spelling.

Other mnemonics have variable usefulness. 'There is *a rat* in *separate*' might help eliminate one common error, but I doubt if 'never eat chips eat sausage sandwiches and raspberry yoghurt' really helps anyone remember how to spell *necessary*.

9) Irresistible

Whether words end in *–able* or *–ible* can be quite difficult to ascertain, especially if you spell primarily from the sound of words. Both *–able* and *–ible* are unstressed syllables, in which, in English, the vowel sound almost inevitably comes to be a soft 'uh' sound (the *schwa* sound in linguistics). So how can we tell these endings apart?

One rule which is often suggested is the following.

- If the root is not a complete word, add *–ible*.
  aud + ible = audible
  Examples: visible, horrible, terrible, possible, edible, eligible, incredible.
- If the root is a complete word, add *–able*.
  accept + able = acceptable
  Examples: fashionable, laughable, suitable, dependable, comfortable.
- If the root is a complete word ending in *–e*, drop the final *–e* and add *–able*.
  excuse – e + able = excusable
  Examples: advisable, desirable, valuable, debatable.

There are some exceptions to this rule: *contemptible, digestible, flexible, responsible, irritable, inevitable*, but exploring this with children can be a very useful investigation, as we will discuss later.

PRACTICAL TASK PRACTICAL TASK **PRACTICAL TASK** PRACTICAL TASK **PRACTICAL TASK**

This activity would be suitable for use with Year 5 or Year 6 children.

Brainstorm onto the whiteboard as many words as possible which end in the sound *–ible* or *–able*. Allow a minute for children to spot that there are two ways of spelling the *ible/able* ending. Can anyone spot the rule?

Explain the rule (but admit that there are exceptions): the *–able* ending is added to words which are complete in their own rights (*manage – manageable; knowledge – knowledgeable*), but words with the *–ible* ending (*horrible; possible*) are incomplete without the ending.

Check the rule with these words. Cover up the *able/ible* ending. When does that leave a whole word?

possible	tangible	transmittable
passable	incompatible	remarkable
salvageable	manageable	incorrigible
rechargeable	terrible	invincible
permissible	changeable	
personable	noticeable	

---

10) Harass

Harass is unfortunately just one of those words you have to know. Looking for parallel words does not really help in this case; as you soon come up with *harry*, which has a similar meaning but unfortunately too many *r*'s.

11) Definitely

Any vowel in an unstressed position can sometimes have the sound linguists call a *schwa*: 'uh'. The result is that many people tend to guess when they hear this sound what letter or combination of letters is needed at this point. Phonically it would be plausible to write *definate, definute*, but *definite* is definitely the right spelling.

The trick is to remember *in-finite*. *Definite* is in a sense the opposite of this. Most people for some reason can spell *infinite* correctly but *definitely* is often misspelt. If you ever forget, think of the word *finite*. Say it to yourself a few times if you're more auditory than visual, *'f-eye-night'*, *'deh-f-eye-night*

Using the word web in Figure 4.2 might also help fix the spelling in children's minds.

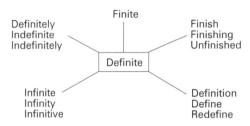

Finite

Definitely	Finish
Indefinite	Finishing
Indefinitely	Unfinished

Definite

Infinite	Definition
Infinity	Define
Infinitive	Redefine

Figure 4.2 A word web around 'definite'

12) Occurrence

Part of the trick of spelling this correctly is to apply the phonic rules we discussed in word 2. It has to be a double *r* because otherwise the *u* would be long: *'ock – oo – rens'*.

More tricky is the decision about *–ance* or *–ence*. Many words end in *–ence* and many in *–ance*. A similar debate concerns the *–ent* and *–ant* endings. Technically the reason for the difference is the Latin origin of these words. As some of you may know (and somewhat fewer care), Latin verbs fall into four basic classes describing their conjugation. In one of these classes of verbs (in fact called the 'first conjugation'), the infinitive forms end in *–are*. In another class, infinitives end in *–ere*. This forms the basis of the suffix rules for most verbs: words derived from first conjugation verbs usually get *–ant* and *–ance*, the rest get *–ent* and *–ence*. But there are exceptions, even to this.

The writer of the Everything web page dealing with this confusion (**http://everything2.com/index.pl?node_id=1528141**) gives the following rules.

Add –ent or –ence, when:

The root ends in soft C or G

- **innocent**
- **reticent**
- **intelligent**
- **tangent**
- **sufficient**

The root contains *–esce*

- **senescent, senescence**
- **putrescent, putrescence**
- **fluorescent, fluorescence**
- **aquiescent, acquiescence**

The root contains *–cid–*, *–fid–*, *–sid–*, *–vid–*

- incident, incidence
- coincident, coincidence
- confident, confidence
- evident, evidence
- subsidence

The root contains *–flu–*, *–qu–*

- sequence, consequence
- fluent, confluent, confluence

The root ends in *–ist*

- existent, existence
- insistent, insistence
- persistent, persistence
- subsistent, subsistence

The root ends in stressed *–er*

- referent, reference
- inference
- deference
- preference

The root ends in *–ere*

- incoherent, incoherence
- adherence, adherent
- interference

And so on.

I have omitted here the many exceptions to each of these rules. Because of this, the complexity of these rules and because it is not particularly useful for most people to have to learn Latin for the sole purpose of spelling words in English correctly, the best advice we can give here is: when in doubt, use a dictionary.

13) Embarrass
Which is the correct spelling: *embarass* or *embarrass*?

If you did not know or were unsure (because they both look sort of right, don't they?) it is *embarrass*. So how do we remember that? Well, there are a couple of ways. First of all you could remember that when you are embarrassed, you go really red (RR – two *r*'s). The second way is to note that there are two *r*'s and two *s*'s, i.e. the letters are doubled. To make it really memorable, why not remember both?

14) Inoculate
Two bits of information can really help here. The first is to know common English prefixes. A prefix is one or more letters or syllables added to the beginning of a word to change its

meaning and the rule about prefixes is that *when a prefix is added to a word, the spelling of the word itself remains the same.* Notice how the following words follow the rule:

commutation	=	*com–*	+	*mutation*
immature	=	*im–*	+	*mature*
misshapen	=	*mis–*	+	*shapen*
misstep	=	*mis–*	+	*step*
underrated	=	*under–*	+	*rated*

If you ignore this rule, it's easy to spell these words without their double consonants.

So, why is it not *innoculate*? Here the second piece of information comes in useful. *Oculus* in Latin meant *bud* (and *eye*) and the word *inoculare* therefore meant to implant a bud into a plant. When in the eighteenth century, scientists discovered that people could be protected from serious disease by having the germs of a milder form of that disease implanted in them, *inoculare* was the word they used to describe what they were doing.

Notice that there are other words, such as *innovate*, in which the second part of their derivation, in this case *novate* (from Latin *novus* = *new*), did start with an *n*. *Innovate* therefore keeps both *n*'s.

15) Weird
We're all familiar with the 'i before e, except after c' spelling rule; but what about the exceptions? Here is a tip to help you remember how to spell *weird*. **We** are **we**ird – we is the beginning of **we**ird.

One website author makes a virtue out of the problem:

> *On the internet you will find a lot of very strange things that will make you think, make you laugh, or make you worry about how much spare time people have on their hands. Some people would call this stuff weird, but it isn't. It is, in fact, wierd. The common spelling mistake of most people on the net has finally developed into a meaning of its own. A hybrid word of wired and weird, it refers to anything weird found through an electronic medium. Pronounced **WHE-URD**, it is something that you will not soon forget.'* (**http://home.pacific.net.au/~turner23/wierd.html**)

PRACTICAL TASK PRACTICAL TASK **PRACTICAL TASK** PRACTICAL TASK **PRACTICAL TASK**

Here are some useful strategies to use when you cannot spell a word. Discuss these with your class, and display the list prominently in your classroom.

1. Break it into sounds (d-i-a-r-y)
2. Break it into syllables (re-mem-ber)
3. Break it into affixes (dis + satisfy)
4. Use a mnemonic (necessary – 'one collar, two sleeves')
5. Refer to word in the same family (muscle – muscular) (word webs)
6. Say it as it sounds (Wed-nes-day) (spellspeak)
7. Words within words (Parliament – 'I AM parliament')
8. Refer to etymology (bi + cycle = two + wheels)

9. Use analogy (bright, light, night, etc.)

10. Use a key word (horrible/drinkable for –able & –ible / advice/advise for –ice & –ise)

11. Apply spelling rules (writing, written)

12. Learn by sight (look-cover-write-check)

A SUMMARY OF **KEY POINTS**

In this chapter, we have set out part of the problem of English words and spelling. It should be clear by now that learning to spell in English is no simple matter, which makes it all the more surprising that most children are well on the way to mastering this by their ninth or tenth birthdays.

We have also hinted at some teaching strategies you might use to help your pupils untangle English spelling in similar ways to our untangling in this chapter. Underpinning all these strategies is that spelling work benefits enormously from being taught in this enquiring manner. As we have seen, correctness in spelling is not always a helpful concept and it is more effective to engage learners in figuring out the vagaries of English spelling for themselves.

Moving on

Have a look at Vivian Cook's Writing Systems website (**http://homepage.ntlworld.com/vivian.c/**). Even the most hardened anti-spelling student will find something of interest here.

RESOURCES

There are a number of very useful websites you will find invaluable in exploring English spelling and its rules.

The Online Etymology Dictionary – **www.etymonline.com/index.php**
This site will give you word origins for thousands of English words and is simple to use.

The Free Dictionary – **www.thefreedictionary.com/**
This is just what it sounds like – a dictionary online. It has the added benefit of being linked to the Free Library of classic works (**www.thefreelibrary.com/**), which contains hundreds of work of classic literature. When you search for a word in the dictionary, you are given examples of where and how this word is used in the classic works in the library.

Wikipedia – **http://en.wikipedia.org/wiki/Main_Page**
This is not just an online encyclopaedia but can also be used as a dictionary and for word investigations. Like all Wikis, it has the benefit that anyone can contribute material to it. This could give children a real incentive to read and find out about words.

FURTHER READING FURTHER READING **FURTHER READING** FURTHER READING

Crystal, D (2006) *Words, words, words*. Oxford: Oxford University Press. A cornucopia of information about words from the inimitable David Crystal. Stimulating enough for your own bedroom reading, but well enough written for you to read aloud sections to your pupils.

Cook, V. (2004) *Accomodating brocolli in the Cemetary: or why can't anybody spell?* London: Profile Books. A thoroughly disorganised book but one of those you want to keep dipping into to uncover more fascinating facts about English spelling (that sounds like a contradiction in terms but this book will change your mind).

5
Working with punctuation

Introduction

Punctuation, on the face of it, is the least interesting aspect of the structure of English texts. Many children find difficulty in learning the niceties of English punctuation: seven- to eight-year-olds do not always reliably even remember to include capital letters and full stops in their writing. Many children leave primary school still not fully conversant with the uses of commas, apostrophes and, virtually universally, colons and semicolons. Indeed many adults, teachers and student teachers included, have problems with these more esoteric punctuation marks. Yet, incredibly, the topic of punctuation spawned, in 2003, a best-selling book (Truss, 2003), with the rather scary subtitle 'The zero tolerance approach to punctuation'. Punctuation, for all its difficulty and abstruseness, clearly intrigues and worries some people.

Yet this interest in punctuation is not reflected in research or writing about the teaching and learning of punctuation. Nigel Hall and Anne Robinson, in the introduction to their book *Learning about punctuation* (Hall and Robinson, 1996), bemoan the lack of research and writing generally about learning to punctuate. This book illustrates its own dilemma, being, as far as we can tell, the only significant publication about punctuation in school in the past 12 years. So, for all the current popular interest in punctuation, advice on how to teach it is very hard to come by. Perhaps a new approach is needed.

In this chapter we will explore English punctuation, as we have other aspects of knowledge about English, through some practical examples of teaching it in classrooms. We will present three case studies of possible ideas for lessons based around a shared text. Each lesson suggestion focuses on a text or texts in which punctuation is used rather differently to modern standard English, and it is through these differences that we will try to introduce the tools to build an investigative approach to teaching punctuation.

The first case study focuses on archaic uses of punctuation. Even in writing little more than 100 years old, punctuation appeared to work in rather different ways to that in modern English text. Primary pupils can profitably be introduced to archaic text (for secondary

English pupils this is a required experience according to the National Curriculum) and there are many interesting features for them to explore, punctuation not least among them.

Case study 2 focuses on punctuation uses in other varieties of English, in this case American writing. Children will increasingly encounter writing from other cultures, especially as the use of the internet spreads, and it can be very beneficial to focus their attention on the ways in which such text operates to apparently different rules to the standard they will be used to.

In case study 3, we will introduce text which uses punctuation more recently developed and still not quite accepted as standard. Many children will be familiar, perhaps more so than their teachers, with writing in newer media such as e-mail, texting, etc., in which punctuation seems to work rather differently. They can profitably explore such new uses as emoticons :-), smilies ☹ and abbreviated text (ROFL – 'rolling on the floor laughing').

CASE STUDY CASE STUDY **CASE STUDY** CASE STUDY **CASE STUDY** CASE STUDY

Study 1

The following extract is taken from the story 'Prince Hyacinth and the Dear Little Princess', from Andrew Lang's *Blue Fairy Book*, first published in 1889. The story concerns Prince Hyacinth, born because of an enchantment with a very large nose, which he, however, thinks is handsome. Hyacinth is searching for his bride to be, the Dear Little Princess, and comes across an old woman – a fairy in disguise. The extract is punctuated here exactly as it was in the original.

'The poor boy is right,' said the Fairy; 'I was forgetting. Come in, then, and I will give you some supper, and while you are eating I can tell you my story in a very few words—for I don't like endless tales myself. Too long a tongue is worse than too long a nose, and I remember when I was young that I was so much admired for not being a great chatterer. They used to tell the Queen, my mother, that it was so. For though you see what I am now, I was the daughter of a great king. My father—'

'Your father, I dare say, got something to eat when he was hungry!' interrupted the Prince.

'Oh! certainly,' answered the Fairy, 'and you also shall have supper directly. I only just wanted to tell you—'

'But I really cannot listen to anything until I have had something to eat,' cried the Prince, who was getting quite angry; but then, remembering that he had better be polite as he much needed the Fairy's help, he added:
'I know that in the pleasure of listening to you I should quite forget my own hunger; but my horse, who cannot hear you, must really be fed!'

The Fairy was very much flattered by this compliment, and said, calling to her servants:
'You shall not wait another minute, you are so polite, and in spite of the enormous size of your nose you are really very agreeable.'

'Plague take the old lady! How she does go on about my nose!' said the Prince to himself. 'One would almost think that mine had taken all the extra length that hers lacks! If I were not so hungry I would soon have done with this chatterpie who thinks she talks very little! How stupid people are not to see their own faults! that comes of being a princess: she has been spoilt by flatterers, who have made her believe that she is quite a moderate talker!'

As an archaic text, this provides us with some insights into the ways in which punctuation conventions have changed somewhat over the course of the past 100 years or so. The following features might be drawn to the attention of a class during a shared reading session using this text.

Examine the uses in the text of the colon (:), a punctuation mark which has fallen somewhat out of favour in modern English. It is used in both the fourth and fifth paragraphs to introduce direct speech, following a verb of speaking (*said*, *added*). It is also used in the final paragraph to link what could have been two discrete sentences together ('that comes of being a princess: she has been spoilt by flatterers').

The first usage is now not appropriate in modern English, and a comma would be used instead. It would also not be correct to begin a new paragraph when direct speech is used in this way. The sentence in modern English would thus read: 'The Fairy was very much flattered by this compliment, and said, calling to her servants, 'You shall not wait another minute...'. What has happened here is that the use of the colon has been replaced by the use of a 'softer' punctuation mark, the comma.

In the second usage, the colon would nowadays be replaced by a 'stronger' punctuation mark, the full stop. This sentence would today be written: 'that comes of being a princess. She has been spoilt by flatterers.'

These two examples illustrate quite well the reason why the colon is no longer as widely used in modern English as it was in the English of the Victorians. As a 'middle-strength' punctuation mark, its territory has been cut away from both sides, and in most cases either the full stop or the comma is now preferred. It should be noted, however, that Lynne Truss, in her best-selling book about punctuation, *Eats shoots and leaves*, rejects this line of thinking about the use of the colon, claiming that its usage is much more complex than as a 'middle-strength' mark between the comma and the full stop.

It can be worth playing around with sentences in order to discover when colons might best be used. Take the following example, which Lynne Truss uses:

> *Tom locked himself in the shed. England lost to Argentina.*
> *Tom locked himself in the shed: England lost to Argentina.*

(N.B. 'Tom locked himself in the shed, England lost to Argentina.' is just wrong, although many pupils might write this way. This is an example of a comma splice; that is, an attempt to join together two completely separate sentences by means of a comma.)

In the first example, Truss argues that the two events described (Tom locking himself in the shed, and England losing to Argentina) are not necessarily related, both simply having occurred at some time. In the second example, however, the colon makes it clear that there is a strong causal connection between the two. Tom is in the shed because England lost. If this argument has any truth, then, for all its gradual disappearance from modern English usage, the colon does seem to have some purpose in the sense of adding meaning to written statements.

Other pairs of sentences to explore with a class might include the following:

> *Our cat likes to sleep. It is his favourite activity.*
> *Our cat likes to sleep: it is his favourite activity.*

Here the distinction in meaning is not so clear. Whatever the punctuation separating the two propositions, there is clearly always a relationship between them. The cohesive tie 'it' makes this clear.

The difference here lies more in the ways in which elements of each of these statements are stressed. For us the stress in the first example comes on the 'It', marking the implication that sleeping, rather than any other activity, is the cat's favourite. In the second example, it feels more comfortable to place the stress on 'favourite', thus emphasising the description of the activity.

These two pairs of sentences illustrate nicely a debate which has raged for some time about the main purposes of punctuation. In the cat sentences, punctuation indicates stress and intonation – what linguists call prosody. In the Tom sentences, however, punctuation clearly indicates different grammatical relationships, and in the end meaning differences.

According to the first view,

> *The different points or stops in punctuation ... are conventional signs designed to show pauses and rests of various lengths in the manuscript ... if the reader is reading aloud, they should help him to pause at the right places for the right period of time, to put the emphasis where it is intended, and to adapt his breathing and the pitch and cadence of his voice to the natural flow or rhythm of the passage.* (Joad, 1939, p59)

Such a view will be very familiar to those of us who remember being taught that, either in reading or writing, a comma indicated 'take a breath'. It also gave rise to what we might term a 'weighting' approach to punctuation – a comma demands a small breath, semi-colons and colons slightly longer ones, while full stops demand the longest breaths of all.

In contrast to this, other writers argue that:

> *Even today there are many who have [an] incorrect, 'resting-place' notion of punctuation; to them the far more important aspects are lost. Nowadays it is considered a misconception to think that whenever you make a pause in reading it is necessary to insert at least a comma. Punctuation has become more logical: there should be a reason for each stop used.* (Moon, 1939, p164)

The logicality, or otherwise, of punctuation usage is the focus of the second of our case studies, in which the attention turns very much to many people's punctuation *bête noire* – the comma (although it will also raise issues surrounding our punctuation of that last French phrase).

CASE STUDY CASE STUDY CASE STUDY CASE STUDY CASE STUDY CASE STUDY

Study 2

The following short text is composed specifically for this book. You might like to show it to a group of Year 5 or 6 children and ask for their responses.

> *My favorite book is J.K. Rowling's "Harry Potter and the Prisoner of Azkaban." My brother told me this book was 'wizard,' a description I would certainly agree with.*

> *We first met Harry Potter in 'Harry Potter and the Sorcerer's Stone.' He is a boy wizard who has to fight the evil Lord Voldemort. Voldemort is supposed to be dead, but keeps trying to come back. Harry has beaten him three times already.*

> *Voldemort does not appear in the 'Prisoner of Azkaban,' so maybe Harry has finally got his 'Keep Out!' sign working properly.*

Most pupils will spot that this text looks slightly odd and some will home in on the spelling of 'favorite' in the first line. Others will point out that the first Harry Potter book was called 'Harry Potter and the *Philosopher's* Stone'. These details indicate that the text is written in American, rather than British, English. You might want to discuss with the children these 'obvious' differences in American English. In the case of the book title, the American version will perhaps seem illogical to them – the creator of the stone in the book not actually being a sorcerer. The spelling difference might seem rather more logical – the 'u' does, after all, carry no sound value in the British spelling of *favourite*. The point to make to them, however, is that language changes and differences are not always subject to laws of logic. Other factors, such as habit, interfere. A really good example of this is to be found in the use in this text of quotation marks and the punctuations surrounding them.

The children should firstly notice the consistent use in the text of double quotation marks. This probably will not seem strange to the children as it is almost certainly the way they will have been taught to punctuate speech and quotations in their own writing. ('Open your speech with 66 and close it with 99.') American printed texts also consistently use double quotation marks to mark off speech and other highlighted elements such as "wizard" in the first paragraph of the text. Yet this is not common practice in modern British printed texts. As an example, here is a brief extract from the original British edition of *Harry Potter and the Philosopher's Stone* (notice we are following our own advice here and we did not write "Harry Potter and the Philosopher's Stone"!)

> *'What are these?' Harry asked Ron, holding up a pack of Chocolate Frogs. 'They're not really frogs, are they?' He was starting to feel that nothing would surprise him.*

> *'No,' said Ron. 'But see what the card is, I'm missing Agrippa.'*

In the American edition of the book, these single quotes become double, to fit standard American printing practice.

British practice is, however, slightly inconsistent in this and there are many British-printed books in which double quotation marks are used throughout. These tend to be older volumes, suggesting that practice in this regard has changed in Britain fairly recently. Thus in an old copy of Arthur Ransome's *Swallows and Amazons* (first published in 1930) we find the following:

> *"Thank you ever so much for bringing the things," said Susan.*

> *"Specially the lanterns," said Titty.*

It is clearly not just taste in girls' first names which has changed over the past 70 years!

The choice of double or single quotation marks brings with it another 'rule' of punctuation which tends to be handled differently either side of the Atlantic Ocean. If a writer wants to include a quote within a quote, he/she cannot write the following:

> *Jenny said "My favourite book is "Harry Potter and the Philosopher's Stone"".*

Nor:

> *Jenny said 'My favourite book is 'Harry Potter and the Philosopher's Stone''.*

Both British and American practice would use a different form of the quotation mark for the outer and inner quoted sections. If you have read carefully so far, you ought now to be able to attribute a country to each of the following versions of this sentence.

> *Jenny said 'My favourite book is "Harry Potter and the Philosopher's Stone"'.*

> *Jenny said "My favorite book is 'Harry Potter and the Philosopher's Stone'".*

It is true, of course, that some writers will prefer to avoid this kind of thing (and especially the rather odd looking ' " which results, by punctuating the sentence differently:

> *Jenny said 'My favourite book is **Harry Potter and the Philosopher's Stone**'.*

One interesting investigation children might do is to search a variety of printed texts to see firstly how quotes are punctuated, and secondly how quotes within quotes are handled. If you provide them with a range of texts, both British and American, they may be able to confirm or reject our hypothesis here that transatlantic punctuation styles are different in this aspect.

Another aspect of the punctuation of our text that some pupils may remark upon is the placing of the commas, and full stops, *vis-à-vis* the quotation marks. The text is in American English and consistently places punctuation marks inside the final quotation marks. This is contrary to standard British English practice. Thus the text has:

> *My favorite book is J.K. Rowling's "Harry Potter and the Prisoner of Azkaban."*

A British writer would write this as:

> *My favourite book is J.K. Rowling's "Harry Potter and the Prisoner of Azkaban".*

Again, where the text has:

> *My brother told me this book was "wizard," a description I would certainly agree with.*

A British writer would write:

> *My brother told me this book was "wizard", a description I would certainly agree with.*

What is going on here? Most American writing style guides, and commentators on written conventions, admit that the British approach is rather more logically based – although this is sometimes expressed in a pejorative way:

> *In American English, the convention is to put commas and periods inside quotation marks. The British follow a more complicated and time-consuming convention, which may be why there is no longer a British Empire.*

> From the North Carolina State University Online Writing Lab
> **//www2.ncsu.edu:8010/ncsu/grammar/**

The logic of the British usage is that the punctuation element (comma, full stop) is attached to the words to which it relates. Thus in the first sentence above 'Harry Potter and the Prisoner of Azkaban' is not in itself a complete sentence. Therefore, in British English, there is no logic in attaching a full stop to it. The full stop, rather, relates to the entire sentence and thus should be placed outside the quotation marks indicating the book title. In the second sentence, the comma indicates the coming adjectival clause, 'a description I would certainly agree with', which is in apposition to the noun it describes. It does not relate directly to 'wizard', but links together the two clauses in the sentence.

In both these cases the American convention is much simpler: the full stop or comma goes inside the quotation marks. The temptation is probably to assume that American style has, over the years, simplified more complex, if more logical, British usage here. This is not actually the case, however. Older British usage in fact placed the full stop and comma inside the quotation marks just like present-day American usage. Over time, it is British English which has moved away from this and injected logic into this aspect of punctuation. This sounds remarkable, largely because we are accustomed to viewing American versions of English as newer than British, and to seeing one of the chief pressures for change in British English as coming from growing Americanisms in films and TV, etc. In fact, as Bill Bryson explains in his wonderful book, *Mother Tongue*, many of the features we associate with American English, such as spelling and punctuation, were in fact present in the British English of the time the American colonies were first set up. One classic example of this is the spelling of words such as *recognise* and *realise*. The spellchecker on our computers, set to UK English, accepts this spelling of these words. If we change the setting to US English, it flags up the words as incorrect and suggests instead *recognize* and *realize*. This seems a straightforward difference until we learn that the house style of Oxford University Press, one of the oldest established of British publishers, insists on the *recognize* and *realize* spellings. The Press explains that this has been its house style since the eighteenth century. In other words, such spellings were exported to pre-Independence America and have been adhered to since: it is British spelling which has gradually changed over the centuries.

CASE STUDY CASE STUDY CASE STUDY CASE STUDY CASE STUDY CASE STUDY

Study 3

The following texts are taken, more or less randomly, from electronic texts of various kinds which we ourselves have either sent or received. Given our ages the innovative punctuation elements we will comment upon in these texts are probably a good deal less radical than those which may be found in the texts of our readers, or of the children they teach. The new electronic media of e-mail, texting and instant messaging are undoubtedly changing our language, and punctuation conventions are only those most obviously affected. A good deal of profitable investigation and discussion can be had by presenting texts such as these to children and asking for their reactions. Our hypothesis, which many teachers would admittedly not agree with, would be that most pupils nowadays are quite aware of the different rules which apply to electronic texts, and rarely try to import these inappropriately to writing in standard forms. But this is a hypothesis which requires active investigation. We simply do not yet know the full effects upon pupils' other writing of their writing electronically.

Text 1: Email
hi there
hows things?
just mailing to wish you happy birthday of yest. hope you got lots of cards and pressies. mines on the way – late as usual I know. hopefully you'll think better late than never.
see you soon I hope.
love and hugs :-)

Text 2: Text
hi, u ok? gr8 2 hr yr news. a job at last! lemme no wen u start. bfn. lol

Text 3: Instant messaging
poshdave: u there?
valiant: howdy. still up?
poshdave: wkin l8 tonite. got summit to finish off b4 tomoro
valiant: wotya doin?
poshdave: just planning a sess for uni. wodya no bout prepositions?
valiant: im workin 2. plannin my lessons.
poshdave: plannins a pain.
valiant: prepositions? like to in out?
poshdave: godda b dun tho
poshdave: yeah those little words
valiant: nuffink im afraid
poshdave: yr no use. go 2 bed!
valiant: cu l8er

Punctuation in each of these samples has clearly been affected by the medium in which the writer is working. There is also clearly an audience effect. All of these texts were written to people who were friends and family of the writers and therefore there is little pressure on the writers to conform to normal standards in these texts. A close friend is not, assuredly, about to criticise you for missing out your capital letters! In fact, of these three media it is probably only e-mail that is likely to be used to communicate with people who are not well known to the writer, and so e-mails will vary in the levels of formality they exhibit.

Punctuation elements are notably very different in each of these three texts from the conventions expected in other written texts. In neither text, for example, are capital letters used. This is simply because to produce a capital letter from a computer keyboard requires hitting two keys at the same time. It is easier, therefore, to ignore capitalisation.

Similarly, there are no examples in these texts of commas or apostrophes. This is probably not because these punctuation marks are difficult to use correctly (although it could be, and they are) but it is more likely that the reason is sheer ease of use. In no case in these texts is the omission of a comma or apostrophe likely to cause a misunderstanding on the part of the person reading them, and so these marks are simply dispensed with. Again, had the e-mail been to someone unknown to the writer, a good deal more care would undoubtedly have been taken in the placing of such marks. The purpose would not have been to enhance the meanings conveyed but rather to leave a particular impression (of competence and carefulness) of the person writing in the mind of the writer. This is an important consideration when thinking about all of the standard conventions of writing, including punctuation. You might discuss this with children by sharing with them (deliberately) badly punctuated draft letters you intend to send to their parents. What impression of you, their teacher, is that likely to make on the parents?

Full stops and other sentence-ending punctuation (!, ?) are handled rather differently in these electronic texts. They do appear, if somewhat inconsistently. Exclamation marks are perhaps used more liberally than would be usual in standard written text, as they help give what is still, in the end, written text some of the prosodic features of speech. In the text, for example 'a job at last!' indicates partially how this would have been pronounced in face-to-face conversation.

Question marks are used more or less in the same way as in standard writing, which is interesting as, at least on our computers, they require the pressing of two keys together, like capital letters. Unlike capital letters, however, their omission might well lead to misunderstandings of the meaning of what had been written, and so they tend to be used.

Full stops are sometimes used where one would expect them to be and sometimes omitted, especially at the end of a contribution ('sentence' is not quite right in these contexts). Again, meaningfulness is the prime consideration. The rationale for punctuation use in these texts thus appears to be, first and foremost, 'Does what has been written convey the intended meaning?' If this condition is satisfied then punctuation need follow no other rules or norms and ease of text entry is the sole criterion.

Electronic texts such as these do also contain distinctive features in terms of their spelling, discussion of which must await another chapter, but also of a completely new system of punctuation known as 'smilies', or, if we are feeling fancy, 'emoticons'. Symbols such as :-) and :-(have become almost universal in electronic text and are now creeping into printed texts as well. Microsoft Word even allows the writer to insert a fuller version of such symbols into a piece of writing – ☹ – and on one of our computers this 'smilie' symbol is automatically produced when a colon, a dash and a right bracket are typed consecutively. This suggests that such symbols are becoming normal in written text and their purpose is the same as the purpose of other punctuation marks – they indicate prosodic features of texts (how you pronounce words and phrases), and they also convey aspects of meaning ('Don't be a wally ☺' means something quite different from 'Don't be a wally').

A SUMMARY OF **KEY POINTS**

What, hopefully, has emerged from this chapter is a clear rationale for teaching and discussing punctuation to and with primary children.

> **Punctuation cannot be presented to them as a set of rules they have to try to learn and adhere to.**
> **The rules change: they have always changed and they are still changing.**
> **The only sensible approach is to open punctuation up as a matter for discussion with children.**
> **There are certain commonly agreed usages within particular writing and cultural contexts and children can best be helped to appreciate these by active investigation of punctuation as it is used within other contexts.**

> > The guiding principle should not be 'You must use punctuation mark X in this way', but rather 'Punctuation mark X can be used in this way sometimes and the effect is Y, and in other ways on different occasions and the effect of this is Z.'

Moving on

Children need to understand that punctuation serves two distinct functions in any written text: on the one hand it gives clues about how the text might have been said aloud; on the other it adds a crucial layer of meaning to a written text. As a final example of this, consider the following two sentences:

Pupils who are taught that punctuation expresses pronunciation and meaning in written text are less likely to use it inappropriately.

Pupils, who are taught that punctuation expresses pronunciation and meaning in written text, are less likely to use it inappropriately.

One sentence refers to all pupils and the other refers only to the lucky ones. Can you work out which is which?

REFERENCES REFERENCES **REFERENCES** REFERENCES **REFERENCES** REFERENCES

Hall, N and Robinson, A (1996) *Learning about punctuation*. Clevedon: Multilingual Matters

Joad, CEM (undated, but probably 1939) *How to write, think and speak correctly*. London: Odhams Press

Moon, AR (1939) *A concise English course*. London: Longmans, Green & Co.

Truss, L (2003) *Eats shoots and leaves: a zero tolerance approach to punctuation*. London: Profile

6
Handwriting

Chapter objectives

By the end of this chapter you should have developed your understanding of:

- **a range of research into handwriting;**
- **the current status of handwriting in UK schools;**
- **the importance of handwriting automaticity for composition;**
- **what constitutes good handwriting;**
- **approaches to teaching handwriting.**

Professional Standards for QTS

Q14

Introduction

We have chosen to include a chapter on handwriting in this book because handwriting is very much the poor relation of the literacy world. It can be seen as a rather unimportant aspect of literacy and many general literacy texts omit it altogether. However, two decades ago important British research in handwriting introduced a strong element of common sense and good practice to handwriting teaching. As a result, most children in the UK learn a simple script which they also see on computers and labels, and which may even help them to spell well.

This chapter aims to revisit established practice in handwriting teaching, emphasising strengths. It also reviews important new research which emphasises that handwriting is actually a language act. This research suggests that, while fluent letter formation and joining remain the first goal of handwriting, it is also vital that children learn to write automatically, so that they do not have to give it any attention. This should be one of our key teaching points, but is currently overlooked and many children may compose less well than they should, because their handwriting is not automatic. This chapter gives suggestions and guidance for handwriting teaching and also reflects on the growing importance of computers for writing.

The current status of handwriting in the curriculum

The most recent survey of handwriting practice (Barnett et al., 2006) collected data from only 39 schools in 2000 and this in itself is perhaps an indication of the status of handwriting. However, this survey found that most of the teachers considered handwriting very important. Despite this, the perspectives on writing that have been popular in schools in recent years have not placed much emphasis on handwriting. In Early Years education, literacy teaching placed the focus of attention in children's writing firmly on the meanings children were able to create. This inevitably created tension between the need to ensure that children developed correct letter formation and the desire to allow them to write freely. The teaching of writing for older children has been shaped by a composition-led view of the writing process which is very much part of the mainstream culture of literacy teaching, at least in England. The National Curriculum for English (DfEE/ QCA, 2000) requires that children be taught to plan, draft, revise, proof-read and present their work, a direct reflection of the process approach, and this is sustained in the Primary Framework (DfES/PNS, 2007). Emphasis upon composing may have drawn attention away from handwriting.

This is reflected in the inclusion of handwriting in the National Curriculum and the Primary Framework for Teaching Literacy. The National Curriculum for England (DfEE/QCA, 2000) deals with the development of movement and style, without any attention to speed or efficiency. The attainment target for writing for children at age seven (level 2) demands that: *In handwriting, letters are accurately formed and consistent in size*. For older children the attainment target for writing at level 4 (the target for 11-year-olds) demands only that: *Handwriting style is fluent, joined and legible*. No mention is made of speed. In the National Test for writing, up to three marks can be awarded for handwriting (of 40) and these are allocated on the basis of a consideration of the formation, orientation and visual fluency of joining in the handwriting of the written pieces. This is an assessment of style. The Framework for Teaching Literacy includes a strand entitled 'Presentation'. This stipulates that at age seven children should:

- **write legibly, using upper and lower case letters appropriately within words, and observing correct spacing within and between words;**
- **form and use the four basic handwriting joins.**

At 11, children should:

- **use different styles of handwriting for different purposes with a range of media, developing a consistent and personal legible style.**

While these are perfectly reasonable age-appropriate targets, they do not address some of the most important aspects of handwriting. This chapter will consider some of the things we do know about handwriting pedagogy and how it can help children's handwriting and composition.

Efficient letter formation and joining – the first priority

In the UK we do not have a prescribed handwriting style. However, each school has a handwriting script and prescribed range of joins. In the last 20 years, almost all schools changed the handwriting script they teach, partly as a result of Peters' research into spelling (1985), which suggested that English spelling was systematic in terms not only of grapho-phonemic regularity, but most significantly in the probability of letters occurring together, offering a high degree of visual regularity. Peters emphasised the link between visual and kinaesthetic learning of spellings and made a strong theoretical case for a link between correct spelling and the use of fluent, joined-up handwriting. By learning the movements of common spelling patterns by hand (kinaesthetically) as well as by eye, it was suggested (Cripps and Cox, 1989; Peters and Smith, 1993) that writers improved their chances of producing correct spellings. The popularisation of this theory in schools through spelling and handwriting schemes coincided with (or caused) a change in the handwriting of children all over the country.

The use of an alphabet including exit strokes right from the beginning of writing teaching, and the joining of letters as early as possible (Cripps, 1988) were the key points of most handwriting schemes. Important research in handwriting at this time (Sassoon et al., 1986) focused on efficiency in handwriting, in particular the efficiency of letter formation, joins and penhold. The key issue identified by Sassoon and her colleagues was that handwriting was a visible trace of hand movements and that the clarity and fluency of handwriting depended on the learning of efficient movements early in the child's writing experience, as ineffective motor habits were very hard to change. The implication of this is that, instead of learning a 'ball and stick' or 'printing' script first, and then a cursive script later (as is still the case in some countries), children should learn a clear, simple and efficient handwriting script, including exit strokes, right from the beginning of writing teaching. By using such a script from the outset children do not have to unlearn inefficient movements such as stops at the end of each letter, and relearn an efficient set of movements for joining. This is why almost every school in the UK teaches a script with exit strokes and many teach scripts with entry as well as exit strokes.

There is less agreement about the degree of joining that should be taught. Sassoon concluded that joining, where comfortable, helped children to achieve fluent and fast handwriting but cautioned against insisting on joins that caused difficult hand movements. Other authors suggested a fully joined script from the beginning of writing, asserting that it assisted in spacing letters, in ensuring correct formation and assisting children in developing a concept of word. Recent research has suggested that, even where children learn a fully joined script they tend to drop the less efficient joins at around age 11 so that they can maximise the efficiency of their handwriting.

REFLECTIVE TASK

Look at two samples of your own handwriting:

- **something you have written for yourself – notes, for instance;**
- **something you have written for someone else to read (it is surprising how much of this will be word-processed).**

How is your 'neat' handwriting different from your own notes?

- – in size;
- – in regularity and orientation
- – in the degree of joining;
- – in the time it takes to produce.

These are key issues for children to learn, so that they can develop an efficient handwriting style as well as a neat form for presentation.

Automatic, fast letter production – the next priority

A key issue emerging from research undertaken over the last ten to fifteen years is the recognition that handwriting is far from a purely motor act. Berninger and Graham (1998) stress that it is 'language by hand' and point out that their research suggests that orthographic and memory processes (the ability to recall letter shapes) contribute more to handwriting than do motor skills (Berninger and Amtmann, 2004). Handwriting is not just about training the hand; it is about training the memory and hand to work together to generate the correct mental images and patterns of letters and translate these into motor patterns of letters – automatically and without effort. If this is the case, then handwriting is an important part of writing, and a language act, rather than just a motor act used to record writing.

Use of working memory is at the heart of writing, temporarily storing all the information necessary for carrying out writing processes. However, working memory can hold only a few items for a short time. If young writers have to devote large amounts of working memory to the control of lower-level processes such as handwriting, they may have little working memory capacity left for higher-level processes such as idea generation, vocabulary selection, monitoring the progress of mental plans and revising text against these plans. It may be that handwriting can 'crowd out' the composing processes we value so much.

One way to manage the limited amount of working memory capacity is to make some processes, such as handwriting, automatic. Automaticity is achieved when a process can be carried out swiftly, accurately and without the need for conscious attention (LaBerge and Samuels, 1974). Some research suggests that automatic letter writing is the single best predictor of length and quality of written composition in the primary years (Graham et al., 1997), in secondary school and even in the post-compulsory education years (Connelly et al., 2006; Jones, 2004; Peverley, 2006). However, we do not know when handwriting typically becomes automatic for children, in terms of age or of rate of letter production.

PRACTICAL TASK PRACTICAL TASK **PRACTICAL TASK** PRACTICAL TASK **PRACTICAL TASK**

This task only works if you cannot touch type automatically.

To experience non-automatic handwriting the nearest experience we can suggest is asking you to copy out a passage onto a word-processor from an unknown book such as the telephone directory. This forces you to keep redistributing your attention and checking in the book. It is very frustrating and indicates how difficult copying and even writing can be for some children.

Our theory, practice and policy in handwriting are underpinned by the assumption that handwriting becomes automatic relatively early on in writers' development, but there is little evidence for this. Scardamalia, Bereiter and Goleman (1982) suggest that handwriting is not automatic until around age ten but Berninger and Graham (1998) offer very convincing evidence that, for many children, handwriting continues to be demanding well into the secondary years and beyond. UK national testing does not assess handwriting speed or fluency and addresses only writing style and neatness. We may be failing to assess an important aspect of writing.

Studies undertaken in Australia (Jones and Christensen 1999; Christensen, 2005) adapted a relatively simple alphabet writing task designed by Berninger et al. (1991) to measure orthographic-motor integration (the ability to generate the mental patterns and motor codes necessary to write letters) and to identify children with automaticity problems. One study measured the orthographic-motor integration, reading and written expression of 114 children in Year 2 (aged seven) before and after an eight-week handwriting programme. More than half the variance in composing scores could be accounted for by orthographic-motor integration, even when reading scores were controlled. Interestingly, the children undertaking the handwriting programme showed significant improvement in their composing skills.

A study of the composition and handwriting of Year 2 children in England (Medwell et al., 2007) showed a very high correlation between children's automatic letter generation and composition, even when reading ability was taken into account. Handwriting automaticity accounted for 34 per cent of the variance in composition for these Year 2 children. This was a much stronger relationship than for speed or neatness. Speed or neatness alone are not enough. It was notable that boys were generally (and statistically significantly) less automatic than girls. The research already demonstrated that boys tend to write less neatly and more slowly. Our goal, then, is to teach children to produce letters automatically so that handwriting is not really an issue for them.

This is a very important finding, given the widespread assumption, discussed above, that handwriting is a matter of presentation. These findings support the suggestion that handwriting is indeed a language act and that orthographic-motor integration, that is automatic letter production, is more significantly related to composition than speed or neatness in the present sample of English children. It may be that improving children's automaticity would help them to compose better. We might also speculate that some children's difficulty with automatic number writing could also hinder them in their written maths work.

PRACTICAL TASK PRACTICAL TASK **PRACTICAL TASK** PRACTICAL TASK **PRACTICAL TASK**

Select a group of children (or even colleagues) from across the ability range in your class. Ask them to do the following timed tasks.

1. Copy out a paragraph from a book as quickly as possible. (Two minutes)
2. Write out the letters of the alphabet in upper and lower case. (As many times as they can in one minute.)

Look at the results of these tasks.

- **Which children wrote most alphabet letters?**
- **Which children copied most text?**
- **Which children wrote most neatly?**

Different children will have achieved at different rates on each of these tests. This should cause you to think about how different writing tasks you use affect children's ability to complete the written task.

Teaching handwriting – good models and lots of practice

Some key issues in handwriting teaching are well known and yet surprisingly easy to overlook. The first of these is the use of a school policy for handwriting. Every school needs to have a school policy and a teacher responsible for helping teachers to use the policy. However, the study by Barnett et al. (2006) suggested that although most schools had a handwriting policy, only around half the respondents felt all the staff in the school used it. This is a major issue when children are trying to develop formation of letters, fluency of joins and automaticity of letter production. All these qualities require clear instruction and regular, frequent practice as well as good, consistent models by teachers.

PRACTICAL TASK PRACTICAL TASK **PRACTICAL TASK** PRACTICAL TASK **PRACTICAL TASK**

Evaluate the models of handwriting you are offering in your teaching. Do you use the school handwriting script:

- **On the whiteboard?**
- **On the electronic whiteboard?**
- **In your marking?**
- **In notices?**
- **In handwriting lessons?**

Think carefully through your last teaching day. How many models of handwriting did children in your class see?

Teaching correct letter formation is, as Sassoon points out, a matter of teaching the correct motion. Poorly formed letters cannot be joined up later, nor can they easily be unlearned. In the EYFS and Key Stage 1 children may learn letter formation as part of learning letter names or phonemes. In either case this is very useful and there is evidence that learning letter shapes helps children's phonological awareness. The use of 'air writing' (often with electronic resources and a mnemonic), painting or chalking large letters, tracing sandpaper letters and making letters in sand, cornflower or jelly are all good ways to begin to establish motor patterns. Later, children can trace and copy increasingly smaller patterns as they gain control of those tricky shapes. Round shapes, in particular, are difficult to form. This is probably why very young children use capital letters so often when they are writing something with an important message. Capitals are much easier to form, especially when you are thinking about things like meaning and spelling.

Handwriting needs to be taught at every level in the primary years. This requires teachers to model handwriting and not just to produce ready-made models – children need to see it happening. The nature of the material to be practised may change in different years of the school but a little, regular practice is important for all children. In Years 5 and 6, this should include speed practice and dictation.

Some children will need more practice than others at handwriting, but almost everyone can develop a fast, automatic hand, even if it is not beautiful. When working with those struggling with handwriting, place the emphasis on automaticity. If you have children with handwriting difficulties you cannot do better than consult Taylor (2001). This publication gives clear guidance on how to assess the handwriting needs of individuals and provide help.

Teaching handwriting – the right equipment

Although children come in all shapes and sizes, unfortunately school tables may be purchased in only one. This means that for every child for whom the table is at the right height, it is at the wrong height for another. Pupils should be able to sit with their feet flat on the ground and their arms well above the surface of the table. The table shouldn't be higher than half the child's height and the chair a third. It may be necessary to use chair pads and different heights of chairs to achieve this. Left-handed children may need to sit a little higher over their writing to prevent them dragging their hands across it. It is also important to make sure that children do not rub elbows while writing (in the case of right- and left-hand writers sitting together). When seated for writing, left-handed writers usually turn the paper to the right and right-handed writers turn it to the left.

Some children, particularly those with writing pain or visual problems, really benefit from writing on a sloping surface, which brings the writing nearer to their eyes, without stooping or straining.

When children begin making those vital hand movements and we want them to learn the trace, they should write with as many media as possible – chalk, paint and fibretips – as large and as small as possible. However, as they go on they will use smaller surfaces – small whiteboards and paper. When writing on paper, graphite pencils provide a lovely blend of friction and smoothness. The fat, triangular ones are great for combining the right amount of 'slip' with a shape that gives a good pencil grip. When children move on to something more permanent, there are really excellent handwriting pens which use a fibre tip to provide good friction and ink flow. Ballpoint pens can be very difficult for children when they use particularly slippery ink to lubricate the ball. Fountain pens are a totally unnecessary evil – design has come a long way since pens were created to imitate the quill. Despite this, the fountain pen continues to exercise a strange fascination for children and for every child who takes to using one effortlessly, there is another who will endure months of inky fingers, lips, pockets and ears. English orthography is designed so that right-handers drag the pen left to right, so a left-hander using a fountain pen is at a disadvantage and may find the nib digs into the paper.

Pen grip is of some importance to young writers. Any tripod grip is acceptable. The only totally inefficient grip is holding the pen barrel in a fist. Left-handed children do best if they hold the pencil a little further from the tip, so that they can see what they are writing. If a child is having difficulty, fat triangular writing tools promote good grip (and are available as pencils, coloured pencils and felt pens).There are plenty of additional grips available and some newer pens have a foam patch built in to assist with pen grip. In cases of very severe motor difficulty, a shaped grip or even a small airflow ball around the pencil helps to promote control.

Assessing handwriting

When assessing any aspect of literacy you need to be clear about your criteria and these will change with the age and experience of the writer. However, throughout primary school you will need to assess the following aspects of handwriting and keyboard writing.

- **Letter formation and movements – does the child form all the letters efficiently?**
- **Fluency of joins – does the child join efficiently?**
- **Orientation and relative size of letters – are letters consistently slanted and are the letters appropriately proportioned?**
- **Placing of letters on the line – are most of the letters well placed on the lines and ascenders and descenders dealt with?**
- **Speed of writing – can the child copy reasonably fast?**
- **Automaticity of letter generation – can the child write dictated text (simple words) reasonably fast?**
- **Keyboard awareness – does the child know the positioning of letters?**
- **Touch-typing – can the child use all ten fingers to type smoothly?**
- **Word-processing – can the child touch-type and use function keys, punctuation, etc.?**

Not all these aspects of writing can be inferred from the written product. To locate formation errors you need to observe the child writing and to estimate copying or dictation you need to time the activities.

Handwriting and computers

For some children handwriting will always be difficult and consume an undue amount of their attention. For these children word-processing is a real relief. Typing on a computer produces very readable, neat text and may free them to compose more freely.

It can be easier to type when you know where the letters are on the keyboard, because there is no complicated motor pattern associated with it. The development of handwriting and word-processing is separate, so some children who are poor handwriters will be good at word-processing. However, there are good reasons why we do not start all children typing form the earliest stages. Learning letter shapes is associated with learning phonological and phonemic awareness and so it is unlikely to be discontinued. As more and more writing will be done, all children will need to learn to word-process. In practice, it may not be necessary for everyone to touch-type but this is a very well automated practice and we believe that all children should learn it from age seven. Unfortunately, if touch-typing is left until later, most children will have had very considerable experience of two-finger typing, through games, networking, etc. which makes learning touch-typing more difficult. The Framework for Teaching Literacy suggests that at seven children should:

- **word-process short narrative and non-narrative texts.**

At 11 they should:

- **select from a wide range of ICT programs to present text effectively and communicate information and ideas.**

This is considerably more than just presentation – it is about choosing the appropriate text or hypertext medium and using it to meet audience needs.

In future, all public examinations will be available on screen and more and more children will complete most of their schoolwork on the computer. The questions which will arise will concern whether or not we should maintain handwriting. As Connelly has demonstrated, undergraduates who do all their work on computer are disadvantaged when forced to do examinations in handwriting, and it is important to maintain automaticity in handwriting. However, at present this is much more for the purposes of notetaking, listing and short missives than for substantial writing tasks and most writing done in a business environment is done through the keyboard.

A SUMMARY OF **KEY POINTS**

> **Handwriting is generally seen as a small part of writing and included (with spelling) in the transcription area of writing.**
> **Composing receives most of the curriculum and teaching attention. National Curriculum and Framework assessment of handwriting is confined to neatness and accuracy.**

> Recent research suggests that handwriting is not just a motor skill; it is a language act.
> Automatic letter generation plays a part in composition and is an underestimated part of handwriting.
> The establishment of correct letter movements and fluent joining is the first priority for handwriting teaching.
> The next priority is automatic letter generation.
> We do not currently know what are acceptable levels of automaticity at different ages but research suggests many children may be able to improve their composition by improving their automatic letter writing.
> Handwriting teaching demands good models, plenty of practice and some basic equipment.
> Successful handwriting teaching requires a school policy and co-ordination.

Moving on

To really understand the handwriting in your current or next school, undertake an audit of the handwriting teaching using the questions below.

1. Write out the school handwriting script (capitals and small letters).
2. At what age do children start joining letters in your school?
3. Do all children in a class start joining at once?
4. Does your school use a particular scheme or set of handwriting teaching materials? (for example, Nelson, A Hand for Spelling, Longman, Cambridge Handwriting, etc.) Yes/no.
5. Which materials?
6. Does your school teach keyboard awareness? Yes/no At what age?
7. Does your school teach touch typing? Yes/no At what age?

School handwriting policy
1. Does your school have a handwriting policy? Yes/no
2. If not, is handwriting included in another policy (such as literacy)? Yes/no
3. How often do children do handwriting practice in your school? [circle one] Daily, a couple of times a week, weekly, less often.
4. How long are handwriting sessions? 0–5 minutes, 5–10 minutes, more than 10 minutes?
5. Describe the pattern of handwriting teaching.
6. Is handwriting linked to other aspects of literacy teaching, like spelling, phonics or reading? Say how.
7. Do the teachers in your school like children to write with a particular type of pen or pencil?
8. Do children practise handwriting on paper that is: [circle one or say which is used at which age] plain paper, lined paper, special handwriting paper with four lines.

Assessment and recording of handwriting
1. How is handwriting assessed in your school?
2. How is handwriting achievement recorded in your school?
3. What intervention or support is given to children experiencing difficulties?
4. What are the features of good or poor handwriting in your school? Examine two handwriting samples and annotate the features.

REFERENCES REFERENCES **REFERENCES** REFERENCES **REFERENCES** REFERENCES

Barnett, A, Stainthorp, R, Henderson, S and Scheib, B (2006) *Handwriting policy and practice in English primary schools*. London: Institute of Education

Berninger, VW and Amtmann, D (2004) Preventing written expression disabilities through early and continuing assessment and intervention for handwriting and/or spelling problems: research into practice, in L Swanson, K Harris and S Graham (eds), *Handbook of research on learning disabilities*, pp. 345–63. New York, Guilford Press

Berninger, VW and Graham, S (1998) Language by hand: A synthesis of a decade of research on handwriting. *Handwriting Review*, 12: 11–25

Berninger, VW, Mizokawa, DT and Bragg, R (1991) Theory-based diagnosis and remediation of writing disabilities. *Journal of Educational Psychology, 29:* 57–9

Christensen, CA (2005) The role of orthographic-motor integration in the production of creative and well structured written text for students in secondary school. *Educational Psychology,* 25 (5): 441–53

Cripps, C (1988) *A hand for spelling*. Cambridge: LDA Publications

Cripps, C and Cox, R (1989) *Joining the ABC: how and why handwriting and spelling should be taught together.* Cambridge: LDA Publications

Cripps, C and Peters, M (1990) *Catchwords: ideas for teaching spelling.* London: Harcourt Brace Jovanovich

DfEE/QCA (Department for Education and Employment/Qualifications and Curriculum Authority) (2000) *The National Curriculum Handbook for Primary Teachers in England: Key Stages 1 and 2*. London: HMSO

Department for Education and Skills/Primary National Strategy (2006) *Primary framework for literacy and mathematics*. London: DES

Jones, D and Christensen, C (1999) The relationship between automaticity in handwriting and students' ability to generate written text. *Journal of Educational Psychology*, 91: 44–9

LaBerge, D and Samuels, SJ (1974) Toward a theory of automatic information processing in reading. *Cognitive Psychology*, 6: 292–323

Medwell, J, Strand, S and Wray, D (2007) The role of handwriting in composing for Y2 children. *Journal of Reading, Writing and Literacy*, 2(1): pp10–21

Peters, M (1985) *Spelling caught or taught: A new look.* London: Routledge and Kegan Paul

Peters, M and Smith, B (1993) *Spelling in context.* Slough: NFER Nelson

Peverley, S (2006) The importance of handwriting speed in adult writing. *Developmental Neuropsychology*, 29: 197–216

Sassoon, R, Nimmo-Smith, I, and Wing, A (1986) An analysis of children's penholds, in Kao, H, van Galen, G and Hoosain R (eds.) *Graphonomics: contemporary research in handwriting*, pp93–106. Amsterdam: Elsevier

Scardamalia, M, Bereiter, C and Goleman, H (1982) The role of production factors in writing ability, in Nystrand, M (ed.) *What writers know: the language, process, and structure of written discourse*, pp173–210. New York: Academic Press

Taylor, J (2001) *Handwriting: a teacher's guide. Multisensory approaches to assessing and improving handwriting skills*. London: David Fulton Publishers. This short, but excellent publication includes a full range of handwriting assessment tools and is ideal for use with children experiencing difficulties. It is clear and well explained.

FURTHER READING FURTHER READING **FURTHER READING** FURTHER READING

Alston, J (1985) The handwriting of seven to nine year olds. *British Journal of Special Educational Needs*, 12: 68–72

Alston, J and Taylor, J (1987) *Handwriting theory, research, and practice*. New York: Nichols

Bentley, D and Stainthorp, R (1993) The needs of left handed children in the infant classroom – writing is not always right. *Reading*, 27: 4–9

Berninger, VW (1994) *Reading and writing acquisition: A developmental neuropsychological perspective.* Dubuque, IA: Brown and Benchmark

Berninger, VW, Abbott, RD, Jones, J, Wolf, B, Gould, L, Anderson-Youngstrom, M, Shimada, S and Apel, K (2006) Early development of language by hand: Composing, reading, listening and speaking connections; Three letter writing modes and fast mapping in spelling. *Developmental Neuropsychology*, 29 (1): 61–92

Connelly, V and Hurst, G (2001) The influence on handwriting fluency on writing quality in later primary and early secondary education. *Handwriting Today*, 2, 5—57

Graham, S and Weintraub, N (1996). A review of handwriting research: Progress and prospects from 1980 to 1994. *Educational Psychology Review*, 8: 7–87

Sassoon, R (1990) *Handwriting: A new perspective*. Cheltenham: Stanley Thornes. This book is a really useful and practical guide to handwriting teaching.

Sassoon, R and Williams, A (1988) *Sassoon primary font*. London: Monotype Imaging

7
Looking closely at reading comprehension

Chapter objectives

By the end of this chapter you should have developed your understanding of:

- **the nature of reading comprehension;**
- **the importance of background knowledge in the comprehension process.**

Professional Standards for QTS

Q14

Introduction

Any examination of the skills of effective reading would place a high priority on the abilities of readers to understand the texts they are reading. Without understanding, or comprehension as it is usually known, readers cannot respond to, analyse, or evaluate a text. Research (see, for example, Pressley, 2001) tells us that comprehending texts is not quite as straightforward as it sometimes appears and many readers, at all ages, have problems with it.

The problems of comprehension

To assess the problem of what to teach when teaching comprehension, we must try to determine what is likely to prevent a reader from comprehending a given text. Or, to put it more positively, what must a reader know, beyond recognising the words, in order to read a text?

We will take an actual example and use it as a guide to the problem. The example text is taken from the first two chapters of *Treasure Island*. We will take eight passages, and attempt to indicate the nature and the source of the trouble a reader might have in reading these passages.

Awkward expressions

I take up my pen ... and go back to the time when ... the brown old seaman ... first took up his lodging at the Admiral Benbow.

One problem readers might have in reading stories is a lack of familiarity with certain idiomatic usage, or modes of expression. Here, the problem is obvious because the expression 'took up his lodging' is an out-of-date phrase. Readers may well know, or be able to figure out, what each word is, but may still be confused. They may not be able to understand what course of action the seaman is following. One aspect of learning how to track characters' actions through a story is learning to recognise the clues that indicate when a character is pursuing a given plan.

Recognising the schema

... took up his lodging at the Admiral Benbow.

Adult readers now realise that the Admiral Benbow is a kind of hotel (or inn, as we are later told). But how do we know that? We know it the same way we know that in 'Sam ordered a meal at the Ganges', 'the Ganges' is a restaurant, probably an Indian restaurant. We, as adult readers, recognise the scenario because we are in what is sometimes referred to as a schema. A schema is a sequence of thinking triggered by a sentence, phrase or word in the text. Some readers, however, particularly those with less experience of the world, may have difficulty in making this association. They may be unfamiliar with the 'stay at a hotel' schema. Even if not thrown off by the awkward phrase 'took up his lodgings', some readers will not be able to work out that the Admiral Benbow is a hotel unless they are familiar with the hotel schema.

Recognising plots and plans

'This is a handy cove,' says he at length; 'and a pleasant sittyated grog-shop. Much company, mate?'
My father told him no, very little company, the more was the pity.
'Well, then,' said he, 'this is the berth for me.

Here, in the context of the story, adult readers will recognise that the seaman is planning to stay at the inn if it is quiet and secluded enough. We assume that he is hiding, or that perhaps something even more sinister is going on, and we expect to be told the reason why later. But do younger readers? In reading stories, it is important to try to determine the plans of the characters we meet. We must learn to question their motives and see the larger picture. This is a very difficult thing for a reader to learn to do. It involves a new point of view. Young readers tend to accept the people they meet at face value. They trust everybody. They do not generally see or look for sinister plans or plots. To develop expertise as a reader they must learn to ask questions like, 'What is odd about this?' and 'What if the sailor is not someone who can be trusted?'

Most, if not all, plots are based on the interaction between characters' plans as they strive to achieve their goals, the blocking of some of these plans and the success of others. Tracking such things in detail may well be beyond a young reader's experience and needs to be learnt. Watching films can help with this as it will certainly introduce viewers to complex plots and sinister plans. But there is a great difference between processing text and processing moving pictures. In reading, many more inferences must be made about what characters actually have done. In films, actions are generally spelt out in visual detail. Understanding that a character has a plan, and inferring the details of his plan, are easy when watching a film because we can watch the plan develop. We see every detail of a character's actions in front of us. In reading a story, we can assess the plot, but we must infer the details.

Background knowledge of characters

And indeed bad as his clothes were and coarsely as he spoke, he had none of the appearance of a man who sailed before the mast, but seemed like a mate or skipper accustomed to be obeyed or to strike.

Would a young reader know the difference between a 'man who sailed before the mast' and 'a mate or skipper'? What comparison is being made here? Without some knowledge of what seamen of this era did, looked like, wanted, and so on, it is difficult to understand this sentence.

Two things are important here. Firstly, if we want to help children understand this story, we need to give them other stories or texts which will provide them with the relevant background knowledge. Secondly, we must also teach children to wonder about the implications of the details of the story. They must be taught to assess the characters they meet, i.e. what kind of person is being talked about here?

Plot development

> *He had taken me aside one day and promised me a silver fourpenny on the first of every month if I would only keep my 'weather-eye open for a seafaring man with one leg' and let him know the moment he appeared.*

The plot thickens. We know that, but do the children? They must understand something of what a plot is, how stories develop, and so on. Again this understanding is based on tracking characters' emerging plans. Who is doing what? What does it mean? How do I know? How might I be wrong? These are questions worth reflecting upon.

World knowledge

> *His stories were what frightened people worst of all. Dreadful stories they were – about hanging, and walking the plank, and storms at sea, and the Dry Tortugas, and wild deeds and places on the Spanish Main. By his own account he must have lived his life among some of the wickedest men that God ever allowed upon the sea, and the language in which he told these stories shocked our plain country people almost as much as the crimes that he described. My father was always saying the inn would be ruined, for people would soon cease coming there to be tyrannised over and put down, and sent shivering to their beds; but I really believe his presence did us good. People were frightened at the time, but on looking back they rather liked it; it was a fine excitement in a quiet country life, and there was even a party of the younger men who pretended to admire him, calling him a 'true sea-dog' and a 'real old salt' and such like names, and saying there was the sort of man that made England terrible at sea.*

To understand this passage, you need to know something of the values and morals of an English town in the eighteenth century. Further, it is most important to know about businesses – inns, in particular – and how they are run. A basic knowledge of commerce is needed here. This story can be understood effectively only in the presence of the appropriate background knowledge.

Recognising important objects

> *'Ah! Black Dog,' says he. 'HE'S a bad 'un; but there's worse that put him on. Now, if I can't get away nohow, and they tip me the black spot, mind you, it's my old sea-chest they're after.'*

This line is the turning point of the story so far. It indicates that there will be a fair amount of plot associated with the sea chest. As it turns out, what is inside the sea chest is the crucial issue in the story. How is the young reader to know this? How do we know it?

We know it because we know about valuable objects, greed, likely containers for valuable objects, and story structure. When we see a particular object in a story, we expect it to be used in the story. We know that, if the sea chest were not destined to be important in this story, the author would probably not have mentioned it in the first place. Young readers may not yet have this sense of what is likely to become important and they will need to be taught to look out for significant objects, and to hypothesise about the likely uses for these objects.

Inferences, beliefs, and reasoning

I lost no time, of course, in telling my mother all that I knew, and perhaps should have told her long before, and we saw ourselves at once in a difficult and dangerous position.

Why are they in a difficult position? For adults, it is obvious. Our heroes possess objects of value that others know about and will want to steal. But this is not necessarily obvious to inexperienced readers. They must be taught to construct relevant chains of reasoning based on beliefs derived from what they have heard so far, and from what they know of life. But, what do readers know of life? Some of that kind of knowledge is taught by stories. Much of it must be taught when, or preferably before, a story is encountered. Readers must learn to work out what is going on.

This analysis of the knowledge that a young reader must bring to the task of understanding a relatively short text suggests the complexity of what teachers often take for granted in readers' reading. It is often felt that, having understood the words in a text, readers can then easily go on to understand the text as a whole. Comprehension is, however, much more complex than this and the majority of children will need some teaching if they are to make the kinds of associations detailed here.

REFLECTIVE TASK

Re-read the first two pages of a novel that you are familiar with. Try to pick out aspects that you think primary children might struggle to understand. In each case, try to be specific about the background knowledge that a reader would have to have in order to comprehend this aspect.

If you were using this novel with a class of children, what preliminary activities might you do with them in order to develop and activate the necessary background knowledge?

Comprehension as envisionment building

As they engage in reading, readers are constantly adding to and elaborating the vision in their minds of a text's meaning. Referring to this as an 'envisionment' will stress the creative process involved here. Envisionments are text-worlds in the mind, and they differ from individual to individual. They are a function of one's personal and cultural experiences, one's relationship to the current experience, what one knows, how one feels, and what one is trying to achieve. Envisionments are dynamic sets of related ideas, images, questions, disagreements, anticipations, arguments and hunches that fill the mind during reading. An envisionment is always either in a state of change or available for and open to change. This act of change is 'envisionment building'. Envisionment building is not just an activity occurring during reading; we build envisionments all the time when we make sense of ourselves, of others, and of the world.

For example, when you meet someone for the first time, let's say at a party, you might have no knowledge of that person except for physical appearance, dress and an assumption that the individual is acquainted in some way with the person who is giving the party. With these first few clues, you begin to build an envisionment of the person (more or less detailed, depending on your interest). You know that the person is a man, fairly young (looks about 20), well dressed, in very good taste, if a bit formal. His reserved manner suggests that he is a private person, perhaps a bit withdrawn. He looks and sounds well educated and professional but is somehow different from the other more mature people also at the party. And so it is that you build an envisionment of who he is. At first your envisionment is filled with a few knowns, some maybes, and a lot of questions. As you glean more information about this person, through conversations with and/or about him, your envisionment develops.

In reading, envisionment refers to the understanding a reader has about a text, which is also subject to change as ideas unfold and new ideas come to mind. During reading, envisionments change with time; as more of the text is read, some ideas become less important, some grow in prominence, some are added, and some are reinterpreted. Even after the last word has been read and the book closed, the reader is left with an envisionment that is subject to change. Changes can occur through writing, additional thought, other reading, or discussion. Envisionments grow and change and become enriched over time, with thought and experience.

We can think of envisionment building as an activity in making sense, where meanings change and shift and grow as the mind creates its understanding of a text. There is a constant interaction (or transaction, as Rosenblatt (1978) calls it) between the person and the text, and the particular meaning that is created represents a unique meeting of the two. An envisionment is not merely visual, nor is it always a language experience. Rather, the envisionment encompasses what an individual thinks, feels and senses, sometimes knowingly, often tacitly, as she or he builds an understanding.

But what happens across time that causes our envisionments to change? As we read, we develop new thoughts. Some earlier ideas, questions and hunches no longer seem important or pertinent to our understanding. Yet other ideas have begun to assume prominence, and draw new questions and hunches from us. From this perspective, an envisionment represents the total understanding a reader has at any point in time, resulting from the ongoing transaction between self and text. During the reading of any particular book or play or chapter, a reader has a 'local' envisionment, which changes as new thoughts (from the text, from the reader and from other people and events) lead to changes in overall comprehension. In this way, a local envisionment evolves into a 'final' envisionment that is not the sum of what we thought along the way but is a modified envisionment resulting from all the changes in the local envisionments that have led to this one. Some ideas from previous envisionments remain in the final envisionment, but other parts are gone – no longer critical to the meaning of the text. Each local envisionment is qualitatively different from the one it replaces; it is not a tree trunk with layers of its past within it but rather a butterfly that is essentially unique at each new stage of life. Even after the last word is read, we are left with an envisionment that is also subject to change with additional thought, reading, discussion, writing and living.

Comprehension as schema building

REFLECTIVE TASK

Read the following passage which, unless you have a background in nuclear physics, you are likely to find difficult to understand. Think a bit about exactly what it is about the passage which makes it difficult to understand.

> *Ilya Prigogine has demonstrated that when an 'open system', one which exchanges matter and/ or energy with its environment, has reached a state of maximum entropy, its molecules are in a state of equilibrium. Spontaneously, small fluctuations can increase in amplitude, bringing the system into a 'far from equilibrium' state. Perhaps it is the instability of sub-atomic particles (events) on the microscopic level that causes fluctuations on the so-called macroscopic level of molecules. At any rate, strongly fluctuating molecules in a far-from-equilibrium state are highly unstable. Responding to internal and/or external influences, they may either degenerate into chaos or reorganise at a higher level of complexity.*

You probably found it difficult to understand or remember much of this passage for the simple reason that it makes little sense to you. What is it that makes it difficult?

People commonly attribute difficulty in understanding texts to the difficult words used. This passage certainly has many obscure words which do cause difficulty. Comprehension, however, relies on something a good deal deeper than just knowledge of vocabulary. To see this, read the next passage and try to make sense of it.

> *The procedure is actually quite simple. First you arrange things into different groups. Of course one pile may be sufficient depending on how much there is to do. If you have to go somewhere else due to lack of facilities that is the next step, otherwise you are pretty well set. It is important not to overdo things. That is, it is better to do too few things at once than too many. In the short run this may not seem important but complications can easily arise. A mistake can be expensive as well. At first the whole procedure will seem complicated. Soon however, it will become just another facet of life. It is difficult to foresee any end to the necessity for this task in the immediate future, but then one can never tell. After the procedure is completed one arranges the materials into different groups again. Then they can be put into their appropriate places. Eventually they will be used once more and the whole cycle will then have to be repeated. However, that is a part of life.*

In this passage there are no difficult words, yet it is still very hard to understand. However, once you are told that the passage describes the procedure for washing clothes, you can understand it perfectly easily.

What really makes the difference in understanding text is the background knowledge of the reader. If you have adequate previous knowledge, and if you realise which particular knowledge the new passage links with, then understanding can take place. This background knowledge can be thought of in terms of structures of ideas, or schemas (Rumelhart,

1980). Understanding becomes the process of fitting new information into these structures. This process is so crucial to understanding text that it is worthwhile spending a little time considering exactly how it works.

PRACTICAL TASK PRACTICAL TASK **PRACTICAL TASK** PRACTICAL TASK **PRACTICAL TASK**

Look at the following story beginning:

The man was brought into the large white room. His eyes blinked in the bright light.

Try to picture in your mind the scene so far. Is the man sitting, lying or standing? Is he alone in the room? What sort of room is it? What might this story be going to be about?

Now read the next extract:

'Now, sit there', said the nurse. 'And try to relax.'

Has this altered your picture of the man or of the room? What is this story going to be about?

After the first extract you may have thought the story would be set in a hospital, or perhaps concern an interrogation. There are key words in the brief beginning which trigger off these expectations. After the second extract the possibility of a dentist's surgery may enter your mind, and the interrogation scenario fade.

Each item you read sparks off an idea in your mind, each one of which has its own associated schema, or structure of underlying ideas. It is unlikely, for example, that your picture of the room after the first extract had a plush white carpet on the floor. You construct a great deal from very little information.

Comprehension in reading is exactly like this. It is not simply a question of getting a meaning from what is on the page. When you read, you supply a good deal of the meaning to the page. The process is an interactive one, with the resultant learning being a combination of your previous ideas with new ones encountered in this text.

As another example of this, consider the following sentence:

Mary ran indoors to get her birthday money when she heard the ice-cream van coming.

Without trying too hard you can supply a great deal of information to the meaning of this, chiefly to do with Mary's intentions and feelings, but also to do with the appearance of the van and its driver's intentions. You probably do not immediately suspect him as a potential child molester! Notice that most of this seems so obvious, we barely give it much conscious thought. Our schemas for everyday events are so familiar we do not notice it when they are activated.

Now compare the picture you get from the following sentence:

Mary ran indoors to get her birthday money when she heard the bus coming.

What difference does this make to your picture of Mary, beyond the difference in her probable intentions? Most people say that she now seems rather older. Notice that this difference in comprehension comes not so much from the words on the page as from the complex network of ideas which these words make reference to. These networks have been referred to as schemas, and developments in our understanding of how they operate have had a great impact upon our ideas about the nature and teaching of reading comprehension.

It appears that if new knowledge is intelligible within the schemas already existing within the mind, then it will simply be absorbed into these schemas, expanding them but not fundamentally altering their nature. This process is known as assimilation.

Sometimes, however, new knowledge conflicts in some way with that already in the mind. Then the existing schemas will need to be altered in some way to take account of the new information. This process is known as accommodation.

As an example of both assimilation and accommodation in action, take the case of going to a restaurant. Imagine that, while visiting a new city, I go to a restaurant that I have never been to before. How do I know how to behave, what to expect from the waiter, the order of courses I might receive, how to order my food? I know these things from my restaurant schema, which has been built up over the course of many years from all my previous experiences with restaurants. My experience in this particular restaurant simply adds to my schema, being assimilated into my existing knowledge.

Imagine, however, if my new experience is rather more radically different from previous experiences. Suppose I have never been into a Japanese restaurant before and this evening will mark my first visit. The first thing I will notice is that much of my previous restaurant knowledge does not apply in this case. The restaurant certainly looks different than others I have visited, the decoration and even the seating arrangements being new to me. The tables are laid very differently, the plates and cutlery are different. When it comes to the menu, this is so distinctive (even in a different script) that I will need a lot of help interpreting it from the waiter. The order of courses is different, as are the expectations of what I might drink during the meal. In a whole host of ways this experience challenges my existing restaurant schema, yet it is still distinctly a restaurant that I have entered. I need to adjust my schema quite a lot to take account of this new experience, accommodating my mind to encompass this within the new restaurant schema I take away with me.

These twin processes of assimilation and accommodation are constantly at work as readers read new material for understanding. Comprehension rests upon this active engagement of the reader with new ideas.

A SUMMARY OF **KEY POINTS**

In this chapter we have:

> **explored some of the complex nature of what is usually referred to as 'reading comprehension';**
> **suggested that understanding text is not a simple business but rests upon the ways in which previous knowledge, stored in the mind as schemas, is brought to bear to make sense of new information.**

Moving on

The obvious next step to take here is to think about some practical ways to teach comprehension to your learners, building upon the insights you have gained from reading this chapter. You will find several suggestions for classroom activities in the next chapter but you would also find it extremely useful, and interesting, to visit the University of Connecticut Literacy Web at **www.literacy.uconn.edu/compre.htm** where you will find an enormous range of teaching ideas and materials, as well as links to the research papers which back them up.

REFERENCES REFERENCES **REFERENCES** REFERENCES **REFERENCES** REFERENCES

Pressley, M (2001) Comprehension instruction: What makes sense now, what might make sense soon. *Reading Online*, 5(2). Available at **www.readingonline.org/articles/art_index.asp?HREF=/articles/handbook/pressley/index.html**

Rosenblatt, L (1978) *The reader, the text, the poem: the transactional theory of the literary work*. Carbondale, Ill.: Southern Illinois University Press

Rumelhart, D (1980) Schemata: the building blocks of cognition, in Spiro, R, Bruce, B and Brewer, W (eds) *Theoretical issues in reading cognition*. Hillsdale, NJ: Lawrence Erlbaum

8
Approaches to developing comprehension

Chapter objectives

By the end of this chapter you should have developed your understanding of:

- **the nature of reading comprehension;**
- **the problems of simplistic approaches to teaching reading comprehension;**
- **a range of teaching approaches which can develop comprehension.**

Professional Standards for QTS

Q14

Introduction

In her analysis of reading as a transaction, Louise Rosenblatt (1978) distinguishes between the text and the poem. By the *text* she means the set of marks on the page; by the *poem* she means the transaction that occurs as readers bring their past experience to bear on the text to create meaning. The poem, therefore, is not a thing but a process, not an object but an event. Moreover, it is a continually changing process. When a reader reads a story for the second time, his/her prior knowledge includes what is remembered from the first reading. Thus the second reading is not merely a reiteration of the first but a new process that takes its form partly from the reader's knowledge of the first reading.

A similar change occurs when readers hear or read other people's ideas about a story they have read. Because we bring our own set of experiences to the text our individual reactions are not likely to be identical to someone else's: we each create our own 'poem' as we read the text. But hearing someone else's reactions to and ideas about that story will affect our next reading of it, whether or not we accept or value that other person's view. As an example, imagine a child reading *The Lion, the Witch and the Wardrobe* as a simple adventure story. If during class discussion someone compares the death of Aslan with the death of Jesus, the child may reread the text with that idea in mind, and the second reading will be significantly affected not only by the first reading but also by the interpretation suggested during the class discussion.

Take another example. *Anne of Green Gables* tells the story of a rather wild but enchanting orphan girl who is brought up by her elderly brother (Matthew) and sister (Marilla). Students who reread this story as part of their teacher training course usually remember how, as children, they identified with Anne. Now, as adults, they find themselves more in sympathy with Marilla. Nothing in the text has changed. The words on the page are the same as those they read 10 to 20 years earlier. The changes have occurred in the reader.

What also has an impact, of course, is the reader's purpose, which affects their response. A child, a librarian responding to a parent's complaint about a book, a literary critic, a proof-reader and the author's mother are all likely to read a text for quite different purposes – which will influence their responses to and interpretations of this text.

Implications for teaching

This transactional view of interpretation and understanding presents a serious challenge to traditional approaches to teaching, and assessing, comprehension.

One very common approach to teaching comprehension has been that of supplying readers with a text to read, and following the reading by the asking of questions, in a written or oral form.

REFLECTIVE TASK

As an example of this approach, consider the following. Read the passage and try to answer the questions below it.

> *The chanks vos blunging frewly bedeng the brudegan. Some chanks vos unred but the other chanks vos unredder. They vos all polket and rather chiglop so they did not mekle the spuler. A few were unstametick.*
>
> *1. What were the chanks doing?*
> *2. How well did they blunge?*
> *3. Where were they blunging?*
> *4. In what ways were the chanks the same and in what ways were they different?*
> *5. Were any chanks stametick?*

You should have found it reasonably easy to provide acceptable answers to these questions, but you will certainly feel that you do not, even now, understand this passage. What is a chank, and what were they doing?

You are able to solve language problems like this because you are a competent language user, and are able to apply your intuitive knowledge of language structures to the task. You know, for example, that the answer to a 'How well ...' question will usually be an adverb (even if you do not know the actual grammatical term), and you also know that most adverbs in English end in '-ly'. If you can solve problems like this, there must be a possibility that primary children may also be able to, especially as it is reasonably well established that most children are themselves competent language users by the age of seven. This casts grave doubt on the effectiveness of comprehension exercises as a means of developing or assessing children's abilities to understand their reading. What has completing an exercise like this taught the reader? Sadly, what many children learn from experiences like this is that reading is not about interacting meaningfully with a text, but really about getting the questions right, which, as we have seen, they can often do without understanding.

Fortunately there are some alternative activities which can be used with children which are much more likely to involve real understanding. The transactional model of reading suggests that comprehension develops through reflection and rereading. Consequently, useful activities will focus on one or more of two phases of reading.

- **Presentation: listening or reading.**
- **Reflection and re-examination: sharing impressions (drawing, talking, writing, acting, moving) and reconsidering the text.**

Activities focused on the second phase, arguably the most crucial of them all, should encourage the learner to return to the text. It is reflecting upon stories and rereading them, perhaps several times, that will develop the learner's understanding. During these return visits to the text the transactions occur, and comprehension develops.

Presenting the text

Shared reading

Shared reading has become a very widely used reading activity. It involves the collaborative reading of a text with a group or class and is included in this chapter because, in essence, it is an activity which begins with a meaningful text. Because the text is presented to the children collaboratively, the initial emphasis can be upon its meaning and their responses to it. Teaching children how the text works – how it is structured, how its sentences link together, how its words are constructed, and so on – can then be done within the context of this meaning.

An important part of shared reading is the demonstrations the teacher can give of how reading works in general and how to read this text in particular. Some examples of these demonstrations are:

- **reading aloud with fluency and expression;**
- **showing the class how an experienced reader deals with difficulties in the text – what readers do, for example, if they reach a word/sentence/paragraph which they cannot understand;**
- **talking about the structure of the text – what the introductory paragraph does, how characters and settings are introduced and developed, how plot lines are advanced.**

A key aspect to shared reading is to gradually get children more and more involved in the reading of the text, but always with the support of other collaborators. Such social support can help the development of confident and fluent reading and lessens the chances of children failing. A shared reading session might start with the teacher reading the text aloud to the group. It could also involve the group reading in unison, individuals reading short sections, or the group rereading a section whose reading has been modelled for them by the teacher.

There are a number of points to bear in mind when doing shared reading with a group.

What kind of text to use?
A range of enlarged texts will be needed, including stories of various kinds, information texts and poetry, so that the children are able to see and hear text at the same time. These texts should have a variety of formats, lively and interesting content and they should ideally be appropriate for extended use over three or four days in a week. Big Books are the most obvious form of text to use, but it is possible to enlarge texts in other ways. Some texts can be enlarged up to A3 size using a photocopier. It is also possible to retype some texts on a word processor and then to print out this text at 48-point size. Some technological aids can also enlarge text, such as an overhead projector. Or you can always use the interactive whiteboard.

What level of difficulty should texts be?

The texts used should be within children's comprehension levels but, ideally, beyond the independent reading level of most of the class. They should therefore provide a challenge and be suitable for extending the children's skills.

With a mixed age class, the difficulty levels of the texts used will need to be varied so that all children can experience an appropriate challenge on a regular basis but no children are continually at frustration level in the reading.

What is the teacher's role?

The teacher needs to take a number of roles:

- to read the text with (not simply to) the class;
- to model reading behaviours such as sound–symbol correspondence and directionality;
- to teach basic concepts about print, such as book, page, word, line, letter;
- to teach and allow children to practise phonic and word-recognition skills in context;
- to show children how knowledge of sentence structures and punctuation can be useful reading strategies;
- to model how understanding occurs through thinking out loud about the text as it is read;
- to show how to try to make sense of difficult words and ideas in a text;
- to help children infer unknown words from the surrounding text and to confirm these by looking carefully at their spelling patterns;
- to target teaching at a wide range of reading ability in the class by differentiating questions to stretch less able children as well as providing further reading opportunities and revision for others.

What is the child's role?

The child's role is to participate in the shared reading, individually and in unison, so as to learn and practise reading skills in the context of lively and interesting texts. The key word here is 'participate'. Shared reading is not an effective teaching strategy if it simply involves a teacher reading aloud to a group. The group have to be actively involved in creating and discussing the reading.

Shared reading can be used as the starting point for a range of other work aimed at extending children's reading skills. Vocabulary work, for example, will often link directly to the text used in the shared reading session. Words from that text can, for example, be used as starting points in the following contexts.

- Generating synonyms and antonyms – Ben's fantasy dog in *A Dog So Small* (Phillippa Pearce) was tiny. What other words do we know for 'tiny'? What words mean the opposite of tiny?
- Defining words and applying them in new contexts – at the beginning of *The Hodgeheg* (Dick King Smith) we are told that Auntie Betty has 'copped it'. What does that mean? Can you use it in another sentence? Is it an example of formal or informal language? What do we mean by 'slang'?
- Exploring how writers can make up new words to express ideas that would previously have taken several words – in *Alice through the Looking Glass* (Lewis Carroll), Humpty Dumpty explains some of the words in *The Jabberwocky*, e.g. 'mome' means 'from home'; in *Little Wolf's Book of Badness* (Tony Whybrow) Little Wolf ends his letters with new ways of saying goodbye – 'Yours tiredoutly'.
- Investigating how new words are added to the language – in *Goodnight Mister Tom* (Michelle Magorian), the word 'blitz' is used. Where does this come from?

These sessions can also create opportunities for direct teaching about the structures, orga-nisation and purpose of vocabulary aids such as the dictionary and the thesaurus. They provide the teacher with opportunities to model the use of such aids and teach their use.

Guided reading

Guided reading is an activity that enables children, in a small group setting, to practise being independent readers. In particular, its aim is to enable children to use a range of reading strategies in combination to problem-solve their way through a text which they have not read before and which has not yet been read to them.

Guided reading is founded on the notion that reading is a multi-strategic process. When we read we are using a variety of clues to work out the meanings of the marks on a page (or screen). These clues are usually referred to as cue systems and include the following.

- **Knowledge of individual words. Research has shown that adult readers actually recognise the majority of words they read without needing to use any other information.**
- **Knowledge of the letters in words and the sounds usually attached to those letters. English spelling is not as regular in its way of linking sounds to letters as many other languages, although, if we take the major units of words as syllables, or onset–rime divisions, English is more regular than if we use the phoneme as the basis.**
- **Knowledge of the grammatical structures possible within words and within sentences. The morphology of English makes many words decipherable even if you do not know them. If, for example, you know the word 'port' the system allows you to work out 'report', 'porter', 'reporter', 'import', 'important', etc. Knowledge of sentence grammar also helps you work out words. In, for instance, the sentence, 'The teacher asked his pupils to write during a history lesson on papyrus', even if you do not know the word 'papyrus', you can work out that it must be some kind of writing surface.**
- **Previous knowledge of the topic of a text gives a lot of clues about the words in that text. Some specialised words are only found in particular contexts, other words have different meanings depending on the context in which they are found. You would, for example, interpret the sentence 'What is the difference between these two?' differently if it occurred in a mathematics textbook or if it occurred in an art book.**
- **Knowledge about the type of text that you are reading can also influence the way you read it. Nobody reads a telephone directory in the same way as they read a poem, even though there are poems that are written in a similar list-like way.**

To be a fluent reader demands the control of all these cue systems. As fluent readers read they are constantly drawing upon all these sources of knowledge. In fact, for fluent readers, there is usually too much information available for reading – we tend to use only a fraction of it because we do not need all the cues available. This is the principle of redundancy in reading. There are many ways of deriving meaning from our reading but we only actually make use of a very few at once. Children, however, are not as practised or as competent at reading and need teaching to use the whole range of cues available.

Organising a guided reading session

Guided reading works best with a smallish (five or six) group of children who are roughly at the same stage in their reading, and with a text which they would generally be able to read on their own but which does provide some challenge and some area of difficulty which creates an opportunity for new learning. They need a copy of the text each, plus one for the teacher. Most picture books and chapter books can be good guided-reading books. Non-scheme books can be graded, for easy management, using systems such as Individualised Reading or the Reading Recovery grades or pre-graded scheme books can be used.

The introduction to the session takes the form of a conversation between teacher and children about the text. The aim of this conversation is to cover the knowledge that will be needed for the children to be properly prepared to read the text for themselves. This knowledge will, naturally, vary according to the text and to the reading development level of the group. The following examples illustrate an introduction for children at an early stage, one for more advanced readers and one for a very advanced group.

Introducing a guided reading session for beginner readers

- **Talk about the title – what do they think the story might be about?**
- **Relate the theme of the story to the children's own experience, e.g. if the story is about a dog, do any of the children in the group have a dog at home?**
- **Introduce the characters in the story, e.g. 'This is a story about two bears and their names are Big Bear and Little Bear'.**
- **Look through the book at the pictures, discussing what seems to be going on in those pictures.**
- **In conversation about the book, use some phrases or words that will be helpful to children in their reading of the book, e.g. in introducing 'Let's go home, Little Bear', you might talk about some of the things Little Bear thinks he hears while pointing to these words on the page.**

Introducing a guided reading session for a group of readers who have some independence and confidence

A group further on in its development might need a less extensive introduction.

- **Introduce the book and give them an overview, e.g. 'This story is called Farmer Duck. It is about a duck that has to work terribly hard on a farm because the real farmer is too lazy.'**
- **Use the pictures selectively, e.g. 'Let's look at what's going on in the first few pictures.'**
- **Give a cue to help children with an unusual phrase: 'Look at the lazy farmer, just lying there in bed. All he does is lie there and ask the duck, "How goes the work? How goes the work?"' (N.B. Use the phrase but do not specifically point out those words on the page. If you feel you need to make the cue more explicit, you might ask the children to find those words on the page.)**
- **Tell the children about something they will be able to find out when they read the book for themselves. 'When you read the book you'll find out how the duck makes the lazy farmer get out of bed.'**

Introducing guided reading to a group of more able or experienced children

A more advanced group (e.g. a group of average Year 2 children) might need the briefest of introductions, e.g. 'This book is called Elmer Again. We've read a book about Elmer before. Who can remember what happened?'

After the introduction

After concluding the introduction to the text, the children should be asked to read it to themselves 'in a quiet voice' and to use their fingers to point to the words as they read. The teacher needs to watch the children as each one reads and note any hesitancy in their reading (the finger pointing will help to keep a check on this). The teacher should not intervene immediately any difficulty is encountered but should be ready to do as soon as it is judged that a child needs some additional prompting.

This basic approach can be modified for readers at an early stage of development. Instead of introducing the whole book in one go, the teacher might choose to guide their reading on a page-by-page basis, for example:

- giving the pupils an introduction to a page of text;
- asking them to read that page for themselves;
- giving them an introduction to the next page;
- asking them to read that page for themselves.

Finally they can go back to the beginning and again independently reread the whole book, this time in one go.

The activity can be concluded in a variety of ways.

- Discussing the text just read with the group.
- Rereading the text in unison. The purpose of this is for the teacher to model reading with expressiveness and pace.
- Setting a follow-up activity based on the guided reading text.

Guided reading with older children

With older children the focus of guided reading changes and the teacher's time and attention should be aimed not at enabling the children to practise independent reading, but at enabling them to analyse text, fiction and non-fiction, at a deeper level. The focus might particularly be on plot, character, setting and dialogue in fiction texts.

The purpose of guided reading at this level is to help children to develop more complex responses to texts, supported by references to what they have read, and to help them to take account of the views of others. The aim is to help the children:

- develop deeper and more complex responses to text;
- make inferences from subtle textual cues;
- evaluate character motivation and the author's intentions;
- analyse the way in which authors create particular effects through their use of vocabulary, grammar, textual organisation and other stylistic devices.

In guided reading all children will need to have a copy of the same text. This might be a complete text, perhaps a short story or a poem. Or it might be an extract, perhaps an excerpt from a novel. Sometimes the group might be reading the whole book over a number of weeks, a chapter at a time.

It is beneficial, in teaching literacy, to make close links between reading and writing. Through the discussion in guided reading sessions children can develop an explicit knowledge about text and its characteristic features, including its structures and styles. This might then lead to them writing in the particular genre for themselves.

Teaching example

The following example illustrates how a guided reading session with a group of Year 5/ 6 pupils led first to group discussion and then to individual writing tasks.

The group began by reading to themselves the following extract from *The Wizard of Oz* (Frank Baum).

When Dorothy stood in the doorway and looked around, she could see nothing but the great grey prairie on every side. Not a tree nor a house broke the broad sweep of flat country that reached to the edge of the sky in all directions. The sun had baked the ploughed land into a grey mass, with little cracks running through it. Even the grass was not green, for the sun had burned the tops of the long blades until they were the same grey colour to be seen everywhere. Once the house had been painted, but the sun blistered the paint and the rains washed it away, and now the house was as dull and grey as everything else.

(A cyclone picks Dorothy's house up and carries it away to the Land of Oz.)

The cyclone had set the house down, very gently – for a cyclone – in the midst of a country of marvellous beauty. There were lovely patches of greensward all about, with stately trees bearing rich and luscious fruits. Banks of gorgeous flowers were on every hand, and birds with brilliant plumage sang and fluttered in the trees and bushes.

After they had read the extract the teacher then discussed the following points with them.

- How did the first part of the description make them feel? Why?
- How did the second part of the description make them feel? Why?
- What did the author do to create such a contrast?

Then they were given the task of rewriting both sections of the passage to reverse this contrast. This was discussed with the group for a while and several examples of possible changes suggested. After writing their changed versions, the group then presented their work to the rest of the class during a plenary session.

Independent reading

Although shared and guided reading are extremely useful approaches to encouraging an interactive approach to understanding fiction text, there are also times when children should be encouraged to read independently. It seems logical to suggest that children will not become avid readers unless they are given opportunities to actually read. The same argument applies to almost any activity. Although I may learn to drive a car during a dozen or so lessons, I do not become a driver without much more opportunity to practise. For many children opportunities to engage in pleasurable reading regularly occur at home, and for these children the supportive atmosphere of a home which values books and reading is probably sufficient to ensure that they too will come to share these values. For others, though, school may represent the most extended opportunity to read that they get, and so it is vital that it does actually give them this opportunity.

RESEARCH SUMMARY RESEARCH SUMMARY **RESEARCH SUMMARY** RESEARCH SUMMARY

The single factor most strongly associated with children's reading achievement, more than socio-economic status or any instructional approach, is the time they spend actually reading (Krashen, 1993). Research has shown that the amount of leisure reading children do is correlated with their reading achievement. In one study (Anderson, Wilson and Fielding, 1988) it was found that children who were very high-achieving readers spent five times as long every day in reading books as did children who were classed as average readers. Reading promotes reading – the more children read, the more their vocabulary grows, the more words they can read, the more reading they can do.

It seems clear that allowing children to read independently for a short time – perhaps only 15 to 20 minutes – during the school day can contribute powerfully to their language and literacy development. This activity is given a variety of names: sustained silent reading (SSR), drop everything and read (DEAR), uninterrupted sustained silent reading (USSR), everyone reading in class (ERIC) or sustained, quiet, uninterrupted, individual reading time (SQUIRT). Most versions of the activity have common features.

- **They often involve everyone in the class reading – including the teacher, who does not take advantage of the time to mark books, hear readers, tidy his/her desk, etc., because that would indicate to the children that reading, while important, is not important enough for the teacher to do it too.**
- **They often occur at the beginning of school sessions, either morning or afternoon. This indicates to the children that the teacher places high importance upon them. Having them at the very end of the day might give the children the message that they were just winding-down times.**
- **They often involve the whole school. In some schools even the headteacher, the caretaker, school secretary and dinner ladies read at these times. This again indicates to the children how important these times are.**

There are a number of other strategies for encouraging children to read independently.

Buddy reading

Buddy reading gives children rather less support in reading than shared or guided reading, but more than having to read completely independently. It involves pairs of children reading together. These may be pairs of similar ability or weaker and stronger students together. It may also involve pairs with three or more years separating their ages. The aim of the activity is for each child to read softly to the other, taking turns with paragraphs or pages. The job of the listening student is to help with any difficulties the reader has. After the reading, the pair discuss what they have read.

If there is a large age gap between the pupils, then an alternative way of managing buddy reading is to get children to use 'echo reading', that is, the older child reads a sentence, paragraph or page, which the younger then tries to read in exactly the same way. This can be an excellent way of encouraging both children to think about intonation and expression in reading.

Reader's theatre

The reader's theatre activity offers a way for readers to participate in repeated readings in a meaningful and purposeful context. Rather than performing in a traditional play where the actors have costumes, props, and have to memorise their lines, in reader's theatre children read aloud from a script using their voices and facial expressions to share the story. This format provides an opportunity for children to develop fluency in reading through multiple readings of a text, using expressiveness, intonation and inflection.

Reader's theatre scripts can be written by teachers themselves, based upon a story they may have already read to a class. There are also plenty of scripts freely available for teachers to download from the internet. American children's author, Aaron Shepherd, for example, has a website devoted to reader's theatre where he supplies lots of scripts suitable for children aged 8 to 15 (**www.aaronshep.com/rt/index.html**). A collection of scripts for younger children, including lots of choral poems can be found at the reader's theatre website (**www.readerstheatre.ecsd.net/collection.htm**).

Using audio books

Recorded books can be a valuable tool for motivating readers, giving them supported reading practice and at the same time providing a model of good reading. Children can listen to a story on cassette while following along in their copies of the book. While listening to the story over and over again, they learn to associate the spoken word with the printed word. Not only does listening to tapes enrich vocabulary and word recognition, but it also provides the listener with reading that is fluent, accurate and expressive. Listening and following along in the book focus on interpretation and allow the reader/listener to become involved in the story.

RESEARCH SUMMARY RESEARCH SUMMARY **RESEARCH SUMMARY** RESEARCH SUMMARY

A number of research studies have found positive effects from the sustained use of audio-taped books. Carbo (1978) reports her work with slower readers in which she found that the use of audio-taped books, as long as they contained readings at a slow enough rate, did enhance the abilities of readers to engage with the texts they were using. Topping and his colleagues (1997) found that the use of audio-taped books significantly enhanced the reading skills, and motivation towards reading, of a range of primary school children, a result confirmed by Byrom's (1997) smaller-scale, but more detailed work.

Many teachers have invested in listening centres for their classrooms where groups of up to six children can listen to the same recorded story while following the text in a copy of the book.

Reflecting on the text

There are a wide range of activities which encourage readers to reflect upon the text they have just read (or had read to them). In the following section I will describe several of these activities but it is important to stress at this point that these are not merely a 'smorgasbord' of activities to be used indiscriminately. Each activity should only be used if it is appropriate for a particular group of children and a specific text.

If each of the activities which follow is to be used effectively, it is also important for teachers to understand the transactional nature of reading, as discussed earlier. The implication of this is that there will rarely be a 'correct' answer in the following activities (although there will be incorrect ones). The key intention is to get children to reflect upon what they have read and make sense of it in their own terms and in collaboration with others. All these activities should involve a great deal of discussion, and it is with talking about books that we should begin.

Book talk

Aidan Chambers (1993) has written powerfully about the importance of talk about books, and the 'reading conference' has become an established part of teaching practice in American and Australian schools. Talking about books, with other children or with adults, gives readers the opportunity to test out their ideas about the meanings of a story, and also to develop these ideas as they encounter those of others.

In some classrooms, groups of children regularly meet in 'literature circles' to discuss their reactions to the stories they have read or had read to them. Literature circles work best when there is no written outcome – if the point of the circle is to produce a piece of work then that is what children will focus on doing rather than exploring tentative ideas about a story. This is not to say that the group cannot be asked to focus upon specific things in their circle meeting: it can be very useful to ask them to discuss questions.

- **Who was your favourite character in the story, and why?**
- **Did the story end as you thought it would? How else might it have ended?**
- **Was the setting important in this story, or could it have been set anywhere else?**
- **Did the story make you feel happy/sad/relieved?**
- **What other stories have you read by this author? Did you like them as much as this one, more, or less?**

Although written outcomes will generally not help get the best out of children during literature circle work, there are, of course, many activities in which they do have a place.

Collaborative stories

In this activity, children are asked to create their own stories in response to a version of a picture book which has had the text removed. This requires collaboration between the original and the new (child) author. The strength of this activity is that it gives readers the opportunity to create meaning at the text level. In doing this, they become more aware of story structure and character development, rather than just sentence and word meaning. It also has the advantage that it can be used to introduce children to texts well beyond their usual reading levels.

The activity needs a no-text version of a picture book. This can be created in a number of ways.

- **Real picture books can have their text covered with correcting fluid or white masking tape.**
- **Sticky notes or strips of paper can be placed over the text.**
- **The text can be covered and pages photocopied or scanned into a computer then printed (this has the advantage that, with a colour printer, illustrations can retain their colour).**

The teacher first shares the original story with an individual, group or class. With less skilful readers, the teacher can read it to them, whereas more proficient readers might read it themselves. Once the text has been read (not necessarily the same day), the children are ready to produce their own versions. They may decide to reproduce a similar story using their own language (without looking back at the text), or to try to produce a completely different version of the story. When this has been done, they then share the new text with other readers. Some might then like to go back to the original text to see how the new text is different.

A useful variation of this activity is to use the pictures from a story which the children have not seen before. Although this changes the nature of the lesson, they still have to use a similar knowledge of language to construct the text. What this variation offers is complete freedom from the constraints of the original text stored in children's memories.

Text sequencing

This involves cutting up a text into pieces (using logical divisions based on meaning) and presenting the text segments to small groups of four to six children. As with the previous activity, it requires the reader to create meaning at the text level. In particular, children need to use their knowledge of story structures.

To use this activity a text of 200–500 words is ideal. It is better if the text is typed or scanned as this enables it to be reformatted so that children do not simply rely on clues such as the section beginning with a sequence of words which physically fit the gap left at the end of the previous section. The focus should be on meaning and text structure rather than physical clues. It is useful to glue the segments of text onto pieces of cardboard of uniform size and to then distribute these among the group. The group is then asked to try to reconstruct the text. At first the teacher might need to help them by asking questions such as *Who thinks they have the first part? Why do you think that piece comes next?* However, it does not take long for most children to learn how to negotiate the activity without assistance.

As a variation to this activity, it can be useful to provide the group with one or two blank cards (deliberately leaving out sections of the text). The group must also place the blank cards in position and write the missing text segments themselves.

Story retelling

The essential purpose of this activity is to get children to reconstruct a text that will then be shared with a larger audience. The text may have been read to the group by the teacher or it could have been read independently. Following the reading of the story, the children are asked to provide a verbal retelling of the story, with props to support their presentation. For example, they might use silhouettes on an overhead projector, a time line, dramatisation, mime, puppetry, etc. By encouraging them to experiment with other methods of making meaning, they are then able to share the meaning they have created with other children.

Character profiles

Character profiles are a simple device to focus readers' attention upon the personalities of specific characters in a text. Their use encourages children to consider not only the personality traits of the character, but the relationships between different characters. Although the composition of the character profile sheet can vary, the format shown opposite is particularly useful.

One way of using character profile sheets is for the teacher firstly to demonstrate filling one in, using a character that all the children are familiar with, preferably one from a piece of literature they have recently read. They then compile their own profile of a different character from the current class story, working either individually or in small groups. They can then be given the opportunity to share these with other members of the class. This is not only extremely enjoyable, but it gives them a chance to hear how others have represented the same, or a different, character from the same book.

The profile sheet can obviously be changed simply by adding or deleting specific categories of information. For example, they might add categories like 'favourite TV programme', 'how he/she spends his/her spare time', 'last seen', and so on. The profile could also be changed into a 'Wanted' poster, and then displayed around the room.

A character profile outline

Name of character:
Picture
Age:
Description:
Special features:
What was he or she trying to do in the story?

Never-ending story

This activity integrates reading and writing. Children are provided with the beginning of a story which they must continue to write, until they are told to pass the story on to another child for it to be continued. The activity requires reading and writing in an interactive way: first reading, then writing, reading, then writing, and so on. It also requires the reader/writer to construct meaning for extended texts (both through reading and writing). Each time a new text is passed on to the next child, it is necessary for him or her to read the text that has already been written, predict what the author was trying to create and plan how to extend the text. In a sense, this activity forces the reader to 'read like a writer' in a way difficult to achieve simply through conventional writing lessons.

It is useful to introduce this activity by modelling it on an overhead projector. After displaying the beginning of the story (selected from any piece of literature), the teacher then writes the next section of the text. After writing several sentences he/she stops, reads the text out aloud, and asks the group to suggest what might come next. Someone's suggestion is then written as the next section of the text. The activity continues in this way until the text is completed to the group's satisfaction.

When children do this activity, it should be explained that they will only be given a limited amount of time to write something, and that they will then have to pass it on to another writer. Ideally, the activity should be used with groups of four to eight children. The story's beginning should only be two or three sentences long. It should introduce a character, set a little of the scene, and perhaps even provide some initiating event. Each child in the group receives a copy of the story's beginning, and is then asked to start writing. After about three minutes, they pass the text on. Once each piece has been finished, it is returned to the person who started it and it is then shared with the whole group.

Story maps

Story maps are graphic organisers that can be useful in helping a reader analyse or write a story. They focus on the elements of the story including the important characters (their appearance, personality traits and motivations), the setting of the story (time and place), the problem faced by the characters, how the problem is approached, and the outcome.

There are many types of story maps that examine different elements of the story.

Some simply summarise the beginning, middle and end of a story.

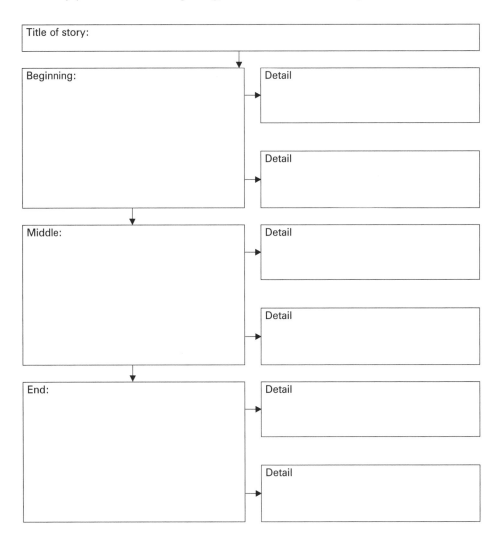

Some focus on the setting, characters, problems, event and resolution of the story.

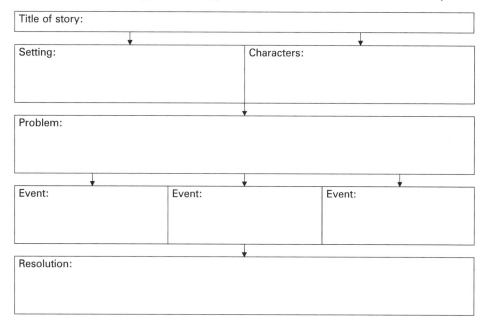

Some list the 'five Ws': the who, when, where, what and why of a story.

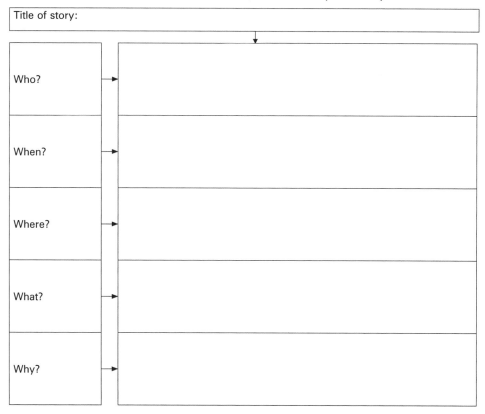

Conclusion

The strategies outlined in this chapter show that there are alternatives to traditional comprehension exercises. Although these activities are all different, they share many common features.

1. They help readers to create meaning as they encounter texts.
2. They require readers to construct a coherent understanding of whole texts.
3. They encourage the use of other forms of meaning-making (such as writing, drawing, dramatisation, etc.) to create a more complete understanding of the text that is read.
4. The teacher is vitally involved as a facilitator, modelling and demonstrating strategies that effective readers use to make sense of texts.

These ideas are not meant to be exhaustive. Rather, they are meant to act as examples of the types of strategies that can be planned to develop comprehension. The way teachers use these ideas, and the alternative strategies that teachers themselves develop, will vary depending upon the text being read, the children being taught and the context within which the lesson takes place. It is important that this should be so. The ideas outlined must never become activities that are ends in themselves. The focus must always be upon the book or story, not the strategies that the teacher is using to help the children get inside the book.

A SUMMARY OF **KEY POINTS**

In this chapter we have:

> **examined the problems with traditional, comprehension exercise methods of developing reading comprehension;**

> **suggested a range of alternative approaches which are interactive and focus particularly on readers' responses to the texts they read.**

Moving on

Reading comprehension is not just a desirable outcome of reading – it is the whole reason why people engage in reading. In this chapter we have focused largely upon strategies for developing reading comprehension using fiction text (although there is no obvious reason why such activities as shared and guided reading should not also be used with non-fiction texts). You will also need to focus upon children's comprehension of a wider range of texts, including the non-fiction texts they encounter across the curriculum. You will find David Wray's book *Teaching literacy across the primary curriculum* (2006) particularly useful as a source of ideas for work with non-fiction texts.

REFERENCES REFERENCES **REFERENCES** REFERENCES **REFERENCES** REFERENCES

Anderson, R, Wilson, P and Fielding, L (1988) Growth in reading and how children spend their time outside school. *Reading Research Quarterly*, 23: pp285–303

Byrom, G (1997) *An evaluation of audio books as a resource for the failing reader*. Unpublished MEd dissertation. Exeter: University of Exeter

Carbo M (1978) Teaching reading with talking books. *The Reading Teacher*, 32: pp267–73

Chambers, A (1993) *Tell me: children, reading and talk*. Stroud: Thimble

Krashen, S (1993) *The power of reading*. Englewood, Col.: Libraries Unlimited

Rosenblatt, L (1978) *The reader, the text, the poem*. Carbondale, Ill.: Southern Illinois University Press

Topping, K, Shaw, M and Bircham, A (1997) Family electronic literacy: part 1 – Home-school links through audiotaped books. *Reading,* 31(2), pp7–11

Wray, D (2006) *Teaching literacy across the primary curriculum*. Exeter: Learning Matters

9
New texts: new literacies

Chapter objectives

By the end of this chapter you should have:

- **developed your understandings about the range of texts, including traditional and digital texts, which children need to encounter to develop their literacy in today's world;**
- **begun to understand some of the key features of digital texts;**
- **considered some possible approaches to developing children's uses of digital texts to enhance their literacy.**

Professional Standards for QTS

Q14

Introduction: What's all the fuss about new technologies?

English teachers, both primary and secondary, have always been very good at encouraging children to engage with, and make sense of, literary texts. From the first introduction of young children to picture story books to the bringing alive of Shakespeare plays with GCSE and A-level classes, working with literature has always been a strength of English specialists. And this work has almost always involved the medium of the book – an excellent, engaging (and portable) way of making texts available to learners.

So, what is all this fuss about new technologies? Does it mean that we should abandon the book as a literary and educational medium? Or does it imply that we have to think about children's reading and writing in new ways?

REFLECTIVE TASK

You might want to spend some time thinking about these questions, especially the question that concerns the future of the book. After all, there are plenty of commentators who would argue that books will, sooner rather than later, be replaced by other media.

Read, for example, the following extract.

> I recently bought a new laptop computer and acquired an example of what has become known as a Tablet PC. This is different from normal laptops in two main ways: its screen can flip over onto the top of its keyboard, making it a little like a chunky A4 writing pad but with a surface of screen rather than paper; and it comes supplied with a special pen with which I can write on the screen, which then either treats my handwriting as a picture or converts it to computer text. As a machine, it is liberating. I can use it to handwrite notes in meetings, which are then automatically converted to typed text. I have a large collection of electronic books any of which I can

read easily on the tablet screen, so on long train or plane journeys it is like carrying 100 books with me to select my reading from. (The only problem with this is that the battery life is only about 3 hours, but in some modern trains you can actually plug the laptop into a mains socket.)

(Wray, 2006, chapter 9)

Or have a look at the website of Libresco (**www.iliadreader.co.uk/index.htm**) which features the iLiad reader, a machine which is apparently, in the words of the website, *changing the way the world reads. forever.* The iLiad is an electronic book reader which, again according to the website, is set to change the way the world reads with features like:

- **lightweight portability**
- **its clear stable display can be read in bright sunlight**
- **rechargeable battery which gives a full days use**
- **large internal memory and three additional memory slots**
- **screen navigation and annotation using the stylus**
- **ability to read notes into a Word document using Myscript notes (optional extra)**
- **WiFi enablement for convenient connectivity.**

Perhaps, given the advent of such incredible innovations (and we are right now only at the beginning of the development of such machines), we will have to admit that, in the course of the next 10–15 years or so, the book as we have traditionally known it will begin to make way for what are clearly more powerful devices.

What do you think?

When you've thought about the issue, read on to see our views on this.

In defence of the book

Our responses to the two questions posed above: 'Does the advent of new technology mean that we should abandon the book as a literary and educational medium?' and 'Does it imply that we have to think about children's reading and writing in new ways?' are 'No, certainly not' and 'Yes, we have no choice.'

Let us look at the book first of all. People have been predicting the end of the book for a long time. The following prediction is typical.

If by books you mean our innumerable pages of printed paper ... I will frankly admit that I do not believe at all – and the progress of modern electronics and mechanics does not allow me to believe – that Gutenberg's invention will not fall, sooner or later, into disuse.

Although this sounds very modern, it was actually written in October 1894 by Octave Uzanne in a short piece called *The End of Books* (this is available, in the original French with English summary on the website: **www.hidden-knowledge.com/titles/contesbib/lafin/lafindesliv res.html**). Unfortunately for Uzanne's credibility the electronic and mechanical inventions he saw as replacing the printed book were wax phonograph cylinders, then recently invented by Thomas Edison. Uzanne goes on to say that, using such technology, the primacy of the writer would be replaced by that of the narrator. Such a claim prefigures the twentieth-century work of Marshall McLuhan whose 'global village' was founded on the primacy of oral, rather than literate, culture. *Moving from print to electronic media we have given up an eye for an ear*, (McLuhan, 1964, ppxii–xiii).

Such predictions do make us think very carefully about the persistence of the book as a medium of communication. It may be that the ways we use books will change, in the same way that our uses of fountain pens changed with the advent of the word processor. Lienhard (1997) makes a similar point:

> *Electronic books will soon have features you never imagined in paper books. They'll have colored pictures that move, spoken words, and background music. And that's just the beginning.*
>
> *Computer books will invite reader participation. Press a button to look up a word or read a source reference – right on screen. Straight-through story lines will give way to mosaic elements that readers can manipulate. We're already seeing variable story lines in the fancier computer games.*
>
> *As we abandon the limitations of the paper book, the electronic book will become unrecognizably different. It'll become so different that the paper book will have to survive, after all.'*

(Episode 708)

Or, as my wife says, *I'll abandon books when they make a computer screen you can read in the bath!* It is unlikely, then, that books will ever completely disappear from social and educational use.

Technology and texts

Although books are here to stay, they will undoubtedly have to take their place alongside other kinds of texts. And we must not underestimate the powerful presence of such new texts. Gere (2002) makes the important point that digital culture has become such an every-day background feature of life in post-industrial societies that its shape, form and function have been naturalised. His description is telling:

> *We are beginning to cease to notice its presence and how it affects us, or at least take these aspects for granted. We sit in front of our computers at work, surf the net, send e-mails, play games on consoles, watch television that is both produced and, increasingly, distributed digitally, read magazines and books all of which have been produced on computers, travel with our laptops, enter information into palmtops, talk on our digital mobile phones, listen to CDs or MP3s, watch films that have been post-processed digitally, drive cars embedded with micro-chips, wash our clothes in digitally programmable machines, pay for our shopping by debit cards connected to digital networks, and allow the supermarkets to know our shopping habits through loyalty cards using the same networks, withdraw cash from automatic telling machines, and so on. Digital technology's ubiquity and its increasing invisibility have the effect of making it appear almost natural.*

(Gere, 2002, p198)

Even those of us who might wish to dispute the pervasiveness of digital culture would recognise ourselves and our daily lives in these mundane activities. Possibly without wishing it so, digital technologies have become part of the everyday for all of us who live in industrial and post-industrial societies. The naturalisation and invisibility of digital culture must be more so for young adolescents and children who do not have a cultural or personal memory of a time preceding digital culture. They are what Marc Prensky (2005) has called 'digital natives' (we older, less digitally naturalised, citizens being 'digital immigrants' – struggling to absorb a culture which is foreign to us, and being regularly out-thought and out-knowledged by our younger compatriots. What would your first recourse be if you were having trouble loading your iPod, programming the digital TV recorder, or trying to find the right piece of clip-art for a Powerpoint presentation? Mine would always be to ask my ten-year-old son!)

What technology and the new digital culture are currently doing in important ways is extending our ideas of text. The multimodal dimensions of digital texts have challenged the notion of literacy as being principally about words, sentences and paragraphs. These in fact represent only part of what is being communicated in digital texts. There is often a tension between the act of making meaning with written words, and the meaning-making which comes from layout and from other aspects of digital texts (e.g. hyperlinks). When we think about the forms and functions of writing on-screen and the texts and contexts in which digital literacy is situated there are some large shifts of emphasis. Some of these shifts are listed below.

a) A move from the fixed to the fluid: the text is no longer contained between the covers or by the limits of the page. Indeed, when the location of the text is on the Internet, it might actually be unlimited, and a key decision the reader has to make concerns when to stop reading.

b) Texts become interwoven in more complex ways through the use of hyperlinks. There is a complicated 'grammar' of linking that we do not as yet understand fully, yet have to act as if we knew when we are using digital texts. As an example of the complexity of this system, the Slideshare website (**www.slideshare.net/atsushi/the-7-navigation-types-of-web-site**) includes a Powerpoint presentation detailing seven types of navigation on websites. These are explained as follows.

1. Site structure navigation – This navigation shows the site structure and allows users to move along with the site structure.
2. Function navigation – This navigation leads users to the site's functional pages, e.g. a site map.
3. Direct navigation – This navigation leads users to some pages directly.
4. Reference navigation – This navigation leads users to related contents and/or related pages of the current content.
5. Dynamic navigation – This navigation generates dynamic result pages, e.g. a Search form.
6. Breadcrumb navigation – This navigation shows the location of the user and allows users to go back to the upper layer, e.g. HOME > PRODUCTS > KITCHEN > PANS
7. Step Navigation – This navigation shows a sequence of pages and the location, and it allows users to move to the previous, next and any other pages, e.g. <PREVIOUS 1|2|3|4|5 NEXT>.

c) Texts can easily be revised, updated and added to. The advent of texts such as wikis (e.g. Wikipedia) means that anyone can add, delete or revise material. This can be variously seen as democratising knowledge, or allowing textual vandalism to reign. Critics claim that, if anyone has an equal right to edit a wiki page, then there is no way of knowing whether the information they include is reliable or not. Others claim that, because millions of people are able to edit the same page, information that is unreliable, or biased, tends to disappear fairly quickly. This is a debate which is ongoing. A flavour of it can be seen in Mitch Radcliffe's blog at **http://blogs.zdnet.com/Ratcliffe/?p=19**

d) Texts can become collaborative with replies, links, posted comments and borrowing. Blogs, discussion forums and instant messaging conversations are new forms of texts which only exist because they are collaborative. According to the Technorati website (**http://technorati.com/about/**) there were, in September 2007, over 110 million blogs on the world wide web, and over 175,000 new blogs appearing every day. Bloggers update their blogs regularly to the tune of over 1.6 million posts per day, with over 18 updates a second. According to this web site:

> *Blogs are powerful because they allow millions of people to easily publish and share their ideas, and millions more to read and respond. They engage the writer and reader in an open conversation, and are shifting the Internet paradigm as we know it. On the World Live Web, bloggers frequently link to and comment on other blogs, creating the type of immediate connection one would have in a conversation.*

e) Reading and writing paths are often non-linear. In traditional reading, we generally turn the pages and proceed in a single direction (with occasional moves backwards to check on previous text). With digital text, however, readers always have a choice about which direction they move in after reading a particular extract. Often, indeed, there are so many possible directions to go that the choice can be bewildering. For example, as I read the page from the BBC website about ancient history (**www.bbc.co.uk/history/ancient/**), I can count at least 40 links to which I can move next in my reading. This kind of reading puts the reader firmly in control of the order and sequence of text that he/she encounters, so it makes the reader an active contributor to the creation of the text being read. But it is also a reading in which it is hard to relax since the reader has to make decisions all the time.

f) Texts become more densely multimodal (as multimedia allows for a rich range of modes to be used). There are new texts to read in which other means, apart from letters, words and sentences, are employed to convey meaning. This includes means such as:

- **coloured text, flashing text, text which flows into different shapes, disappearing text, text in an incredible range of fonts;**
- **pictures, still and moving, which interact with text;**
- **sounds, from speech to noise, which may simply read the text aloud or may add extra meaning to it.**

New texts, new media

Technology, as well as making possible new forms of text, has also opened up new media of communication. For hundreds of years we relied on two major media for communication – face-to-face speech and words written or printed on paper. At the beginning of the twenty-first century, an increasing amount of our communication through language is taking place via alternative media. If this is happening in the world beyond school, then these media will need to find a place inside school as well.

Some of the new media which are gaining increasing acceptance, and indeed becoming essential to modern life, are:

- electronic mail;
- video conferencing;
- CD-ROM;
- online databases;
- mobile telephones;
- instant messaging;
- online chatrooms and discussion forums;
- blogs;
- the internet generally.

In order to use any of these, we need to become familiar with new vocabulary, develop new skills and expand our ideas about communication.

PRACTICAL TASK PRACTICAL TASK PRACTICAL TASK PRACTICAL TASK PRACTICAL TASK

Test your own knowledge of digital literacy
Try to answer the following questions. You will find the answers at the end of this chapter. If you get them all correct you will score 35 marks and you should be aware that when I tested my 10 year old son on these questions, he scored 24. I wonder if you can do better?

1) What kind of material would you mostly find on YouTube?

2) Do you have to have an Ipod to listen to a podcast?

3) What do the letters MSN stand for?

4) What do the following mean?
  - 2DAY
  - ASAP
  - BRB
  - NE1
  - MMFU
  - SOZ
  - GTG
  - XLNT
  - THX
  - BTW
  - H8
  - GAL

5) What does SMS stand for?

6) What is a wiki? And what is the most famous wiki?

7) What are web logs and what are they better known as?

8) What is an emoticon?

9) Computer games are often written based on movies. What was the first movie to reverse this process?

10) What is a Trojan and why is it probably better to avoid one?

11) Which of the following files can you play on an iPod?

– MP3

– wma

– divx

– MP4

– vob

12) And if you can't play them on an iPod, what would you use?

13) Why is spam not a good thing?

14) Complete the sequence:

3.1 95 98 Me 2000 _____ Vista

15) Can you decipher these acronyms?

– PDA

– GPS

– USB

– DVD-R

New words for old

The vocabulary with which we were brought up as teachers and communicators is gradually being supplemented and replaced by new terms. Look, for example, at the words in each of these two lists.

pencil	return key
pen	delete
rubber (eraser for Americans)	button bar
pencil sharpener	icons
ruler	mouse
carriage return	double click
Tippex	predictive text
Banda	emoticons
stencil	spam

Your familiarity with the words in the right-hand list is a useful test of your awareness of modern communication media. It might be a sobering thought to compare your familiarity with these words with that of the children you teach.

The need for new skills

Each of the new media demands the development of new skills. Many of us will remember the difficulties we had when, in primary school, we were introduced to the pen and expected to use one instead of our familiar pencils. Although roughly similar in shape and operation to the pencil, the pen is a different writing instrument and thus requires slightly different skills. Some of us will still have the blotted books to prove our problems in adapting to this new technology.

The introduction of communication media much less similar to those we were brought up to use than was the pen to the pencil can create even more of a skill problem. A simple example of this is the computer mouse. When computers first became common, many adults struggled as they began to learn to manipulate the mouse. It felt like trying to do several impossible tasks at once and there was a constant fear of 'breaking it'. Children were and are much less inhibited in their use of this tool and absorbed the skills naturally in the course of their computer work. The same is true with more recent communication technologies. Many adults struggle to read, much less compose, text messages on a mobile phone. When I am texting, for example, I still cannot quite bring myself to forget punctuation entirely, so it takes me twice as long to text a simple message as I keep having to switch between upper and lower case letters, and I struggle to find the comma. Young people do not bother with any of this and a text message such as 'c u 2nite don't 4get da booz' would be perfectly easy for them to write and read.

New forms lead to new possibilities

A slightly unexpected result of the development of new media is the way in which these make communication itself rather different. Some examples of this are as follows.

- Word-processed and desktop-published documents enable their author(s) to make much more elaborate choices about content and form, and to experiment extensively with these before finally settling on their end-product. Texts produced on a computer thus become provisional, a fact which obliges writers to take more active control over their production.
- Electronic mail is a much faster means of communication than other written forms. Its speed enables rapid responses between communicators and, because of this, it becomes almost like speaking to someone face-to-face. Writing electronic mail thus begins to resemble speech and the media represents a kind of 'half-way house' between speech and writing.
- An elaborate etiquette has developed surrounding the use of various communication forms. Haste (2005), for example, found that, although the vast majority of teenagers reported that they switched their mobile phones to silent mode (but not off) while in the cinema, they saw nothing wrong with interrupting a conversation with their friends to answer a phone call or respond to a text. Also, many more felt a mobile phone or text was an appropriate means of initiating a relationship than felt they could use it to end a relationship. Social customs for this new communication medium are in the process of emerging.
- Lewis and Fabos (2005) report how the teenagers they studied would regularly conduct instant messaging conversations with over four friends simultaneously. As they say, *This is no easy feat. One look at Abby's videotaped IM exchanges with 10 buddies illustrates how complicated it can be to carry on multiple exchanges at once* (p485). Holding different, but overlapping, conversations with ten people at the same time would be extremely difficult to manage face to face, but somehow the asynchronous nature of the instant messaging environment made this possible for Abby.

So what does all this mean for the teacher of primary English?

There are two clear implications for teachers, particularly English teachers, in the widespread acceptance and use of new technology for communication.

- Teachers with a special interest in language and communication will readily see that, as communication itself changes, so their provision for and teaching of it in their classrooms needs to develop to match these changes. Learners, even of primary age, will increasingly arrive in school with extensive experience of these new forms of communication. Virtually all will have access to such media as video and television, and an increasing number will be familiar with computers, mobile phones and the internet. The information superhighway cannot stop at the door of the classroom. Teachers need to find ways of incorporating new media into their classroom work.

- The new media make possible a range of exciting activities with language and literature. They can actually enhance classroom English work rather than threaten it. However, this is far more likely to happen if teachers adopt imaginative and fresh approaches to their teaching rather than expect technology merely to duplicate traditional approaches.

What might some of these imaginative approaches look like?

Some ideas for working with texts and computers

- Developing a class or school magazine in multimedia and hypertext format. This would incorporate writing in a variety of styles, scanned and digitised pictures and photographs, recorded and sampled sound. These materials would need to be organised so readers could find their own ways around the magazine. The production would need to be planned and executed in collaborative working groups, perhaps with some children in the role of art editor and team, copy-editors and design consultants.
- Writing and designing dynamic poetry on a computer. In dynamic poetry, instead of remaining static on the page, words can move, flash, change colour, etc., to provide further enhancements to the poem's meaning. The poetry may also be illustrated by moving or still pictures and a dramatic reading of it may be recorded and added to the computer presentation.
- Learner-designed 'treasure hunts' using information sources such as CD-ROMs or the internet. These could stem from learners' use of these resources as part of their own information-retrieval activities, such as project work.
- Using online collections of words and phrases (known as 'corpora') to explore word usage with learners. The best known of such collections is the British National Corpus and searches of this can be freely carried out at: *http://sara.natcorp.ox.ac.uk/lookup.html*. Sealey and Thompson (2004) report on their use of such corpora to explore language with primary children,
- Involve learners in researching, scripting, recording and distributing their own podcasts on topics they have investigated in or out of class. Podcasts are audio programmes which are prepared in a form (an MP3 file) suitable for playback on a personal media player or computer.

Conclusion

New technologies are changing the nature of text and therefore changing the nature of literacy. As we experience new literacies in our everyday lives, we need to find ways of adapting to these and using them to best effect. As teachers, we also owe it to our learners' futures to prepare them for the new literacies of today and tomorrow.

A SUMMARY OF **KEY POINTS**

In this chapter we have:

> explored the place of traditional texts amid a world of digital texts;

> looked at the key features of digital texts;

> suggested some possible approaches to developing children's uses of digital texts to enhance their literacy.

Moving on

In this chapter we have had time only to scratch the surface of the issues surrounding the impact of new technologies on literacy and its teaching. You should be aware, however, that the revised Framework for teaching literacy which came into effect in England in September 2007 (**www.standards.dfes.gov.uk/primaryframeworks/literacy/**) has as one its overarching aims that children should be taught to *Read and write for a range of purposes on paper and **on screen*** (emphasis added). Digital text is now officially recognised and needs to feature in your teaching.

REFERENCES REFERENCES **REFERENCES** REFERENCES **REFERENCES** REFERENCES

Gere, C (2002) *Digital culture*. London: Reaktion Books

Haste, H (2005) Joined-up texting: the role of mobile phones in young people's lives. Available at **www.-ipsos-mori.com/polls/2004/nestlesrp3.shtml**

Lewis, C and Fabos, B (2005) Instant messaging, literacies, and social identities. *Reading Research Quarterly*, 40 (4): 470–501

Lienhard, J (1997) *The end of books*. **www.uh.edu/engines/epi708.htm**

McLuhan, M (1964) *Understanding media: the extensions of man*. New York: McGraw-Hill

Prensky, M (2005) Learning in the digital age. *Educational Leadership* 63 (4): 8–13 (**www.ascd.org/authors/ed_lead/el200512_prensky.html**)

Sealey, A and Thompson, P (2004) 'What do you call the dull words?' Primary school children using corpus based approaches to learn about language. *English in Education,* 38 (1): 80–91

Wray, D (2006) *Teaching literacy across the primary curriculum*. Exeter: Learning Matters

Answers to practical task

Test your own knowledge of digital literacy

1) *Videos*
2) *No, any MP3 player will do.*
3) *Microsoft Network, but this acronym is almost universally used to refer to the Microsoft Instant Messaging system (which is now actually called Windows Live Messaging).*
4) *today*
   as soon as possible
   be right back
   anyone
   my mate fancies you
   sorry
   got to go
   excellent
   thanks
   by the way
   hate
   get a life
5) *Short Message Service – commonly known as texting.*
6) *A wiki is computer software that allows users to easily create and edit web pages. Once the page is on the web, anyone can edit, delete or add material to it. The best known wiki is Wikipedia.*
7) *A weblog (better known as a blog) is a website where a user writes regular commentaries on various issues. The closest equivalent in traditional literacy is a*

diary, but blogs are usually publicly viewable rather than private.

8) *An emoticon is a symbol or combination of symbols used to convey emotional content in written or message form. Some examples of text-based emoticons include: :-)   :-(;-) (turn your head sideways to see what they mean).*

9) *Tomb Raider, starring Angelina Jolie as the game character Lara Croft.*

10) *A Trojan is a piece of software which claims to do a certain type of action but, in fact, performs another. It might, for example, claim to act as an efficient searcher of your computer or the internet, while at the same time opening a backdoor into your computer through which someone else can view all the files and data you have on that machine. The data might include personal items such a credit card numbers, which can be stolen and used without your knowledge.*

11) *Yes*
    No
    No
    Yes – on the newer iPods. MP4 files are usually videos.
    No

12) *– wma This is an audio file invented by Microsoft. Some MP3 players will play them but not iPods, which are produced by Apple, a rival company.*
    – divx This is a (compressed) video file format. It will play on a computer with the right software.
    – vob This is a video file format. It will play on a computer with the right software.

13) *Spam is the name given to the unsolicited bulk messages that most people get in their e-mail. On a typical day, I receive around 200 spam e-mails, advertising get-rich quick schemes and other, less savoury, items, each of which takes time to delete. Fortunately I have a spam filter on my computer which deals with most of it, because otherwise it would make e-mail almost useless.*

14) *XP – they are versions of the Windows Operating System.*

15) *Personal Digital Assistant*
    Global Positioning System
    Universal Serial Bus
    Digital Versatile Disk – Recordable

Index

Note. The letter 'f' after a page number denotes a figure.